THE LAZY WEEKEND COOKBOOK

THE LAZY WEEKEND COOKBOOK

Matt Williamson

For Ivy, Grace and Dorothy, who make weekends wonderful.

First published in the United Kingdom in 2018 by
National Trust Books
43 Great Ormond Street
London WC1N 3HZ

An imprint of Pavilion Books Company Ltd

ISBN: 9781911358374

A CIP catalogue record for this book is available from the British Library.

10 9 8 7 6 5 4 3 2 1

Reproduction by Mission, Hong Kong
Printed by Toppan Leefung Printing, China

Senior Commissioning Editor: Peter Taylor
Senior Editor: Lucy Smith
Senior Designer: Gemma Doyle
Photographer: Jill Mead
Home Economist: Henrietta Clancy
Prop Stylist: Linda Berlin

C41.5

This book can be ordered direct from the publisher at the website
www.pavilionbooks.com, or try your local bookshop.
Also available at National Trust shops or www.shop.nationaltrust.org.uk

CONTENTS

Introduction

The weekend is the reward for which we wait (and work) all week. Weekdays tend to hurtle by in a steady blur, all speedy meals and 30-minute suppers. The weekend serves as brilliant respite, demanding that we take our feet off the pedals (and close those screens!) and find a more leisurely pace. Sharing good food, cooked with love and attention, is among the most convivial and pleasurable ways to spend time with friends and family. A kitchen table, picnic blanket or garden bench, laden with dishes, invites us to stop and sit and enjoy a meal together. The food we cook for such occasions should be as varied as it is generous and delicious. All the recipes here are intended to serve 4 people (unless stated otherwise), with scope to scale up or down for your guests.

The recipes in this book are split into the moments and mealtimes that make up the weekend. A good robust brunch, if executed well, should put paid to any lunch plans. Whereas the nimble breakfast eaten on the hop will whet the appetite for a great big sharing lunch. You might also plan an elaborate, knock-your-socks-off Saturday night supper, which should demand enough effort to wow your guests but still afford the time to get some food shopping done for anyone hankering for Sunday lunch.

Blink and you might miss it: with just two days, I find the best approach to weekend cooking is to find a balance. Choose the mealtimes you want to pay particular attention to, and go easy on yourself. You don't want to be cooking all weekend long, do you? There are recipes that will boost your confidence in the kitchen: the Moroccan Spiced Chicken Pie (page 54) is a particular favourite of mine. Fragrant, heady with sweet spices, herbs and dried apricots, this sumptuous pie balances flavour like no other. The crackle of the filo as you slice into the pie is a moment that will have your guests salivating. There are other recipes that, though they require a bit of prep beforehand, will make you look like a kitchen pro when it comes to dishing up. The Easy Dinner Parties chapter is a canny collection of dishes that won't have you breaking a sweat when your guests ring the doorbell. I am a chef and my many years in professional restaurants have taught me that the best dishes are those that effortlessly come together – where the ingredients are the stars of the show – so choose the best quality ingredients your budget allows. Try the Baked Duck Legs with Spiced Plums (page 155) for a dinner party dish that is sure to have everyone asking for seconds. And if you've had a long week and are on your last legs, there are a good few recipes that are easy to assemble and take minutes to make. Rustling up a batch of cheesy Muffins (page 47), to bake while you read the weekend papers, will have you wondering why you don't make them more regularly. Likewise, the Sesame Flatbreads (page 29) are a cinch to make, chewy and moreish.

We are lucky here in the UK to have an enormous variety of food shops. From supermarkets to independent shops on regional high streets, to farmers' markets, National Trust farm shops and online shopping – the diversity of ingredients on offer is impressive and always exciting. For this reason the recipes in this book have a global reach, together with a very British one. Arm yourself with some tasty ingredients, check the weather, phone some friends and plan a barbecue or picnic, or light a fire and cosy up with your family for a hulking great Sunday roast. You could light some candles (don't all good dinner parties have candles?) and invite some guests over for an elegant supper – perhaps even a cocktail or two using the syrups on pages 10–11.

The best weekends are relaxed weekends. You choose – how much do you want to take on? *The Lazy Weekend Cookbook* offers an eclectic array of dishes, encouraging you to cook the food you want to all weekend long.

As with most things, the policy of many hands make light work is never truer than in the kitchen. When it comes to bigger gatherings or family shindigs, accept any help offered in the kitchen, from picking herbs to laying the table or even grating a hunk of cheese – and absolutely never refuse anyone's help when it comes to the dishes! Come Sunday evening, you should have your feet up and a smile on your face. Job done.

BREAKFASTS

Breakfast is where the weekend begins, and is one of the most important meals of the day. While there are certainly days that might see us flinging cereal into a bowl and hurtling out the door, the recipes in this chapter offer a diverse set of dishes to conjure up when time isn't quite so pressing. Eggs rule supreme and a pot of coffee is essential.

Three Pancake Syrups

A fabulous alternative to maple syrup, golden syrup or jam, these flavourful pancake syrups will please your family and impress any weekend guests. Stored in the fridge, these syrups will keep for a good couple of weeks. Serve them with the Pikelets on page 14, whip up your easiest pancake recipe or use to jazz up shop-bought crêpes. And in a cocktail? Now you're talking.

Cinnamon Syrup

Add other spices as you prefer, such as a couple of cardamom pods, or a pinch of ground allspice or grated nutmeg. The aroma as you drizzle this syrup over warm pancakes will send you reeling. This syrup can also be used as the basis for a warming hot lemon drink; add extra lemon juice and hot water to taste. Just the thing if you are suffering from a wintery cold.

MAKES ABOUT 300ml

125g demerara or light
　　brown sugar
50g honey
100ml water
½ tsp ground cinnamon or
　　1 cinnamon stick
Pinch of salt
1 tbsp butter

Put the sugar, honey, water, cinnamon and salt into a small pan and bring to the boil, stirring until the sugar has fully dissolved.

Remove from the heat and whisk in the butter.

Leave to cool slightly, then transfer to a jug for serving or a glass jar for storing.

Honey and Orange Syrup

A sprig of fresh rosemary or thyme can be added as you remove the hot syrup from the heat, to infuse as the syrup cools. Bitter Seville oranges can be substituted, when in season, adding a complex fruity sourness to this syrup.

MAKES ABOUT 300ml

200g honey
Finely grated zest and juice
 of 1 large orange
1 tbsp orange liqueur, such as
 Grand Marnier, Cointreau
 or triple sec, or use rum
 (optional)

Put the honey, orange juice and a splash of water into a small pan and bring to the boil, stirring occasionally until evenly combined.

Remove from the heat and stir in the orange zest and the liqueur (if using).

Leave to cool slightly; it will thicken as it cools. Transfer to a jug for serving or a glass jar for storing.

Blueberry Syrup

This intensely purple syrup brings bags of flavour and colour to your breakfast table. It is also delicious rippled through thick plain Greek yogurt or spooned over ice cream.

MAKES ABOUT 500ml

½ unwaxed lemon (or wash
    a waxed lemon in warm
    water and scrub gently
    to remove wax)
250g blueberries, washed
200ml water
100g white sugar

Peel two strips of peel from the lemon, leaving as much of the white pith behind as possible, then juice the lemon.

Put the berries and water into a saucepan and use a potato masher to crush the berries in the water. Add the lemon peel, lemon juice and sugar and bring to the boil, then lower the temperature and simmer for 10 minutes.

Remove from the heat and leave to cool slightly. Remove the lemon peel and pour into a blender; blend until smooth.

Ladle the mixture into a fine sieve and press with the back of a ladle or spoon to extract as much juice as possible. Discard the solids. Transfer to a jug for serving or a glass jar for storing.

Pikelets

These are very easy: they need little more than a mixing bowl and a frying pan to make. Devoured straight from the pan, dripping with butter and a dollop of jam, these slim crumpets – or tubby pancakes – will soon become a regular at your weekend breakfast table.

MAKES ABOUT 12

150ml milk
150ml hot water
200g plain flour
1½ tsp dried yeast
1 tsp sugar
½ tsp salt
Butter, to cook and serve

Mix the milk with the hot water and leave until just tepid.

In a large bowl, mix the flour, yeast, sugar and salt, then add the liquid and mix well. Cover and leave in a warm place for about 1 hour or until it is bubbling and has risen to about one-and-a-half times its original volume.

Give the batter a very gentle stir, then heat a large frying pan over a medium heat. Grease with a smear of butter and turn the heat down slightly.

Test the batter and pan heat by cooking a generous dessertspoon of batter for about 1½ minutes on one side: it should begin to set and bubbles will appear. (If the batter is too thick, the bubbles won't be able to break through, so gently stir in an extra tablespoon of milk.) Once the upper surface is just set, flip the pikelet over and cook for a further 1½ minutes on the other side, adjusting the heat as required.

Spoon generous dessertspoons of batter into the frying pan to make thick pancakes about 10cm in diameter – you should be able to fit about three or four in the pan each time. Cook as above for about 1½ minutes on each side.

Re-grease the pan and cook the remaining pikelets. Serve while they're still warm, with salted butter and jam.

French Toast – Sweet

Clarified butter (see below) is perfect here as it won't burn in the pan as you cook the eggy bread. You can of course use regular melted butter, but you'll need to watch it carefully.

4 eggs

1 tbsp white sugar, plus extra for sprinkling

1 tbsp plain flour

Large pinch of salt

½ tsp mixed spice

Finely grated zest of ½ lemon

4 thick slices (about 3cm thick) of slightly stale, good-quality white bread

4 tbsp clarified butter (method below), or use melted butter

Break the eggs into a bowl and beat lightly.

Mix together the sugar, flour, salt and spice, then beat into the eggs, along with the lemon zest, until completely smooth. (This can be done in a blender.)

Heat a large frying pan over a medium–high heat.

Dip the bread in the egg mixture for about 20 seconds on each side, until just soft.

Add the butter to the pan, then add the eggy bread and fry for about 2 minutes, until golden and crisp (you might need to do this in batches, adding 1 tablespoon of the butter for each slice of bread).

Carefully flip over and cook for about 1 minute on the other side until golden and crisp, then serve immediately, sprinkled with a little more sugar.

French Toast – Savoury

Follow the recipe for sweet French toast, omitting the sugar and spice. Add a tablespoon of chopped fresh herbs, some chilli flakes, or a couple of tablespoons of grated mature cheese to the egg mix. Salt and plenty of freshly ground black pepper are essential.

Clarified Butter

Easy to make, clarified butter is an endlessly useful cooking fat, as it can be heated over a high heat without burning. You can store it in a covered container in the fridge for a month or two.

Melt about 100g of butter in a pan over a low heat. Skim off any of the frothy residue that rises to the surface. When the butter is a clear golden-yellow colour, carefully pour the clarified butter into a small container, being sure to leave any of the milky residue behind in the pan. You can discard these milky curds or use them in batters or cake mixtures in lieu of some of the milk.

Omelette Arnold Bennett

This recipe is a classic, and for good reason. The story goes that the writer Arnold Bennett was holed up at the Savoy Hotel, penning a novel, *Imperial Palace*, about a grand hotel. The chefs in the kitchen were keen to hone the perfect omelette for the hard-working author. Mr Bennett was evidently very happy with the chefs' endeavours: thereafter, in various hotels throughout the world, he would request that this same omelette be cooked for him. The omelettes can be made individually or, much easier and more convenient to serve a crowd, as one big omelette. Use other hot-smoked fish, such as mackerel or salmon, if you prefer.

400g smoked haddock fillets, undyed is best, skinned and roughly chopped
200ml double cream
200ml milk
2 bay leaves
1 onion, finely chopped
Salt and freshly ground black pepper
Freshly grated nutmeg
4 tbsp butter
2 tbsp plain flour
4 eggs, plus 4 egg yolks
2 tbsp finely chopped chives
30g Parmesan or other hard cheese, grated

Put the smoked haddock into a pan with the cream, milk, bay leaves, half the onion, and some black pepper and nutmeg. Bring almost to the boil, turn down the heat and simmer gently for 2 minutes. Remove from the heat and leave to infuse in the pan with the lid on for a few minutes.

Preheat the grill to medium hot.

Heat half the butter in a saucepan and fry the remaining onion for about 5 minutes, or until soft.

Remove the fish to a plate (it doesn't matter if it breaks up a bit) and strain the fish poaching liquid into a jug.

Add the flour to the fried onion and cook for a couple of minutes, then gradually whisk in the fish poaching liquid and cook until it thickens. Check the seasoning, adding salt and pepper to taste. Whisk in the egg yolks and chives, then gently stir in the fish. Put to one side.

Break the whole eggs into a bowl and whisk well.

Heat the remaining butter in a large frying pan over a medium-high heat. When the butter foams, pour in the eggs and tilt the pan to cover the base, leave for 30 seconds, give a quick stir, then shake the pan to even out the partially cooked omelette.

When it is still a little undercooked, remove from the heat, pour over the sauce and scatter with the cheese.

Put the frying pan under the grill until the top of the omelette is lightly golden and just cooked, then serve immediately.

Revueltos-style Spring Onion and Asparagus Omelette

These Spanish-style eggs are a delicious and versatile cross between an omelette and scrambled eggs. Revueltos will work with pretty much anything you like to serve with your eggs: fried mushrooms, onions or bacon, cooked prawns or smoked salmon, roasted peppers, chopped fresh tomatoes or steamed asparagus. You can omit the bacon, but add a splash more olive oil if you do.

200g thin asparagus,
   woody parts trimmed or
   snapped off
4 large eggs
20g manchego or Parmesan,
   finely grated
Salt and freshly ground
   black pepper
3 bacon rashers, finely
   chopped
1 tbsp olive oil
4 spring onions, thinly sliced

Steam or boil the asparagus until just tender, about 3–4 minutes, then drain well.

Whisk together the eggs, cheese, a large pinch of salt and some pepper.

In a large frying pan over a medium-high heat, fry the bacon in the olive oil for about 4 minutes, until golden brown.

Add the spring onions and fry for 1 minute to soften. Add the cooked asparagus and stir to heat through. Reduce the heat to medium and shake the pan to spread the asparagus mixture in a single layer.

Pour the egg mixture over the asparagus and cook until the eggs have very softly set on the base, then tilt the pan gently and run a rubber spatula around the edge and through the base to allow the uncooked egg to flow underneath.

Give the pan a gentle shake and cook for about 2 minutes, until the eggs are just about set, and even still a tiny bit runny (the eggs will continue to cook in the residual heat). Tilt the pan and slide the omelette out on to a plate to serve.

Huevos Rancheros

This recipe, with the eggs cooked over a piquant tomato sauce, is a one-pan wonder, with minimal washing up. Huevos rancheros can easily be scaled up if your breakfast guests swell in number or appetite. Freshly warmed bread to swoop through the sauce is essential.

2 tbsp vegetable oil

1 large onion, finely chopped

2 garlic cloves, finely chopped

2 peppers (1 red and 1 green is good), deseeded and roughly chopped

1 bay leaf

1 tsp smoked paprika

1 tsp ground cumin

Cayenne pepper or chilli flakes, to taste

2 x 400g tins chopped tomatoes

200ml water

Salt and freshly ground black pepper

400g tin black or kidney beans, drained and rinsed

4 eggs

Flatbreads, tortillas or wraps, to serve

Small bunch of coriander, roughly chopped

Small handful of grated mature Cheddar or crumbled feta

Heat the oil in a large frying pan over medium high heat and fry the onion for about 10 minutes, stirring occasionally, until soft.

Add the garlic, peppers, bay leaf and all the spices and cook for 2 minutes.

Add the tomatoes, water, salt and pepper, then simmer for 10 minutes, stirring occasionally, until reduced to a thick sauce.

Stir through the beans and check the seasoning, adding extra salt and spices as needed.

Use a spoon to make four wells in the tomato mixture and crack an egg into each. Put the lid on and cook the eggs in the sauce for about 4 minutes, until the whites are set and the yolks runny.

Meanwhile, heat the flatbreads or tortillas in a dry pan until lightly toasted.

Scatter the coriander and cheese over the eggs and serve immediately (the eggs will continue to cook in the residual heat).

Texan Breakfast Tacos

Tacos go down a treat at any time of the day; for breakfast they are a revelation. Fuel for the day, up the ante and think big with your flavours. They take a bit of preparation but once you have all of the ingredients ready to go, you will look like a complete breakfast pro to your soon-to-be-converted breakfast-taco devotees.

2 tbsp olive or vegetable oil

200g streaky bacon or chorizo, roughly chopped

200g boiled potatoes, roughly chopped

½ red pepper, deseeded and thinly sliced

Salt and freshly ground black pepper

8 small or 4 large corn tortillas, or wraps

2 avocados, peeled, stoned and diced

2 ripe tomatoes, roughly chopped

Small bunch of coriander, roughly chopped

½ bunch of spring onions, finely chopped

50g butter

6 large eggs, lightly beaten

3 tbsp milk

100g sour cream

Hot chilli sauce, to serve

Heat the oil in a large frying pan over medium high heat and fry the bacon or chorizo until browned and cooked through, about 5 minutes. Use a slotted spoon to transfer to a large bowl, and reserve the fat in the pan.

Add the potatoes and red pepper to the pan, add some salt and pepper, and turn up the heat. Cook, stirring often, until golden brown and crispy at the edges, about 10 minutes.

Meanwhile, heat the tortillas in a dry pan until hot and lightly toasted. Wrap in a damp cloth and keep warm between two plates.

Mix the avocado, tomatoes and coriander together and season with salt and pepper; put to one side.

Add the spring onions and 1 tablespoon of the butter to the potatoes and cook for 2 minutes, stirring occasionally, until the spring onions are soft. Add the potato mixture to the chorizo and cover to keep warm. Return the pan to the heat.

Mix the eggs and milk. Add the remaining butter to the pan, add the egg mixture and cook gently, stirring, until just cooked and lightly scrambled but still loose. Season and take off the heat.

Load up each taco with egg, followed by the potato mix, then top with the avocado mix, the sour cream and the hot sauce.

Maple and Pecan Granola

Making your own granola is a gratifying task. Soon you will find yourself sprinkling the odd handful over yogurt, porridge or chopped fresh fruit, mixing it into your usual muesli, or enjoying a bowlful with milk as a speedy, fuss-free breakfast. Maple syrup adds sweetness to this wholesome mélange of oats and nuts. I've also added a touch of cocoa to bring an earthy dimension to the granola.

MAKES ONE LARGE JAR
(approx. 1 litre)

3 tbsp coconut or
    vegetable oil
1–2 tsp ground cinnamon
    (depending on taste)
4 tbsp pure maple syrup
30g sugar (light brown or
    demerara are nice)
2 tbsp cocoa powder
    (optional)
250g rolled oats
100g pecans, roughly
    chopped
100g almonds, roughly
    chopped
50g sunflower seeds
50g pumpkin seeds
Pinch of salt
200g dried apple, roughly
    chopped (or use raisins
    or dates)

Preheat the oven to 150°C (140°C fan) and line a baking tray with baking parchment.

In a large saucepan, warm the oil, cinnamon, maple syrup and sugar together with the cocoa (if using).

Add the oats, nuts and seeds and stir until completely coated, then spread out evenly on the lined baking tray, sprinkling over a little salt.

Bake for 25–30 minutes, until the mix is golden brown and crisp throughout, turning the tray after about 15 minutes so it bakes evenly.

Remove from the oven and leave to cool, then stir in the dried apple, breaking up the granola to your preferred size as you stir. Store in a large airtight jar.

Frozen Breakfast Smoothie

Frozen berries or chopped fruit – used straight from the freezer – are ever-handy for making breakfast smoothies. The combinations are endless, but for me bananas are a must, lending a natural sweetness to any smoothie. Choose ripe, speckled bananas for maximum flavour. Bee pollen has a reputation as a bit of a superfood – if you struggle to find it, substitute a teaspoon of honey. You can add a couple of ice cubes if you want a super-cold smoothie and your blender is up to the task.

400g mixed frozen berries,
    or other frozen fruit
1 ripe banana, or 5 ripe figs
5 tbsp granola or muesli
100g plain yogurt
400ml milk or unsweetened
    almond or oat milk
1 tsp bee pollen or honey to
    taste (optional)

Place all the ingredients in a blender and blend until smooth. Pour into glasses to serve.

Banana and Walnut Porridge

Perfect porridge every time. Steel-cut oats take slightly longer to cook than rolled oats. The payoff, however, is a porridge with superior texture. I've given measurements in cups as the proportions are simple – use the same cup or container to measure the liquids and the oats. You can use other fruit and nuts to top the porridge, adding more or less sugar or syrup to taste. Instead of bananas, try it with apples stewed with cinnamon or rhubarb stewed with a little ginger.

1 cup water (about 250ml)
2 cups whole milk
1 cup steel-cut or rolled oats
2 tbsp butter, vegetable or
   coconut oil
2 ripe bananas, peeled and
   thickly sliced
2 tbsp brown sugar or
   maple syrup
Large pinch of ground
   cinnamon
4 tbsp chopped walnuts,
   or use another nut
Pinch of salt
Cold milk or cream, to serve

Put the water and milk into a saucepan and bring to the boil. Slowly whisk the oats into the boiling liquid and reduce the heat to low. Cook, stirring occasionally, for about 15 minutes (rolled oats will need less time).

While the oats are cooking, melt the butter or oil in a frying pan and add the bananas, brown sugar and cinnamon. Cook over a medium heat for a few minutes, until the sugar bubbles and thickens, gently turning the banana slices over after a minute or so. Stir through the walnuts and put to one side,

When the porridge is cooked, remove from the heat, cover, add salt to taste and leave to stand for about 3 minutes.

Serve hot, topped with the banana mixture and a small amount of milk or cream.

Baked Spiced Oatmeal

Baking oatmeal makes a surprising and delicious alternative to breakfast porridge. With the oats first soaked overnight, they are then baked and finally given a caramelised sugar crust. You can experiment with the flavourings, adding various fresh and dried fruit, nuts and/or spices. In the unlikely event of any leftovers, slice the bake and warm through on a lined baking tray dotted with a little butter or, more indulgently, fry in a pan with a little butter (clarified is best, see page 15) until crisp and bronzed on both sides.

150g rolled oats

1 tsp ground cinnamon

½ tsp ground ginger

75g almonds, flaked or roughly chopped (or use hazelnuts)

75g raisins (or use chopped dried figs or prunes)

500ml whole milk, plus extra for serving

3 pieces of stem ginger in syrup, drained and finely chopped (optional)

150ml double cream

2 ripe pears (or use apples)

3–4 tbsp demerara or brown sugar

25g chilled butter, cut into small pieces

Cold milk or cream, to serve (optional)

Combine the oats, spices, almonds and raisins and mix well. Stir in the milk and stem ginger (if using) and scrape into a baking dish. Pour over the cream and put into the fridge overnight.

In the morning, preheat the oven to 180°C (170°C fan). Peel, core and slice the pears 1cm thick. Spread over the soaked oats and scatter with 1 tablespoon of the sugar.

Bake for 30 minutes or until the liquid is completely absorbed.

Preheat the grill to its hottest setting. Sprinkle the remaining sugar and the pieces of butter over the baked oatmeal and place under the grill for a few minutes until the sugar and butter have caramelised.

Serve warm with a moat of cold milk or cream.

Quick Sesame Flatbreads with Honey Butter

These flatbreads are easy and quick to make, a versatile family favourite. Serve alongside some fried slices of halloumi for a salty/sweet breakfast feast. Add dried or chopped hard-stemmed herbs (thyme, rosemary or sage) or various spices to the mix – find your own favourite combination. The yogurt in this dough gives a gorgeous milky tang to these failsafe flatbreads.

250g self-raising flour, plus
    extra for dusting
1 tsp baking powder
250g plain yogurt, plus extra
    to serve
4 tbsp sesame seeds
8 dried figs, roughly chopped
    (optional)
Salt
4 tbsp soft butter
2 tbsp runny honey, plus
    extra to serve

Mix the flour, baking powder, yogurt, sesame seeds, figs (if using) and a pinch of salt in a bowl to form a cohesive dough, adding a bit more flour if it's too wet. Cover and put to one side.

Beat the butter and honey together, adding a pinch of salt if the butter is unsalted. Put to one side where it will remain soft.

Tip the dough out on to a lightly floured work surface and dust with a little flour. Knead lightly for 1 minute, then divide into eight equal pieces.

Put a griddle or frying pan on a medium heat.

Dust a rolling pin and the work surface lightly with flour then roll each piece of dough out into a disc about 10cm across.

Cook each flatbread in the hot pan for about 1–2 minutes on each side, until slightly puffy and charred in patches, then put to one side, covered with a clean cloth, while you cook the rest.

Serve spread with the honey butter, with additional honey drizzled over the top and yogurt on the side.

BRUNCHES

Brunch is the mealtime that doesn't really exist during the week, and that is part of its charm. A top-notch brunch should have us waiting in anticipation all week long. Inviting people around for brunch instead of lunch or supper will give a pleasant change of pace to your weekend. Pull out all the stops and plan a brunch party – these recipes are easy to scale up.

Savoury Vegetable Fritters

These little fritters are incredibly speedy to throw together for an impromptu brunch and this is a great recipe to use up any bits and bobs of vegetables (anything you can grate or finely slice, or even sweetcorn) that you might have in the fridge. They match brilliantly with any of the following: chilli sauce, seasoned plain yogurt, cottage cheese or tomato salsa.

150g self-raising flour

3 eggs

50ml milk

50g plain yogurt or sour cream

50g cheese, coarsely grated or crumbled

½ bunch of spring onions, thinly sliced

Small bunch of dill, parsley or basil, finely chopped

400g courgettes, coarsely grated and squeezed dry (or carrots, beetroot, cabbage or a mix of whatever you have)

Salt and freshly ground black pepper

Vegetable or olive oil, for frying

Put the flour in a bowl and whisk in the eggs, milk and yogurt. Stir in the cheese, spring onions, herbs and the grated vegetables. Season with pepper and a pinch of salt.

Heat a frying pan over a medium to high heat and add just enough oil to coat the pan. When the oil is hot, drop in heaped tablespoonfuls of the batter and fry for about 2 minutes, until the bottom has firmed up, then flip over and fry on the other side for 2 minutes. When cooked, transfer to a warmed plate and cover with a cloth.

Continue to make more fritters in small batches, until all the mix is used up. Serve immediately.

Spiced Fruit Muffins

Muffins are at their very best when freshly cooked – cool enough to handle but warm enough to just begin melting the slab of butter that we all know muffins are best served with! Having a muffin recipe in your repertoire – one that you can throw together at a moment's notice – is a great way to get the weekend going.

MAKES 12 MUFFINS

250g plain flour
1 tsp baking powder
1 tsp bicarbonate of soda
2 tsp ground cinnamon
½ tsp ground ginger
¼ tsp ground nutmeg
120g light brown sugar, plus
    3 tbsp to sprinkle on top
250g fresh fruit (apples,
    pears or firm peaches),
    coarsely grated
75g plain yogurt
75g melted butter or
    vegetable oil, plus extra
    for greasing
2 eggs, beaten

Preheat the oven to 190°C (180°C fan) and grease a non-stick 12-hole muffin tin with butter or oil.

Sift the dry ingredients into a mixing bowl, and make a well in the centre.

In a jug or bowl, mix the grated fruit with the yogurt, butter and eggs.

Pour the wet ingredients into the well in the dry ingredients and mix gently, just enough to thoroughly combine the wet and dry, but don't overmix. Spoon the mix into the greased muffin tin and sprinkle the remaining sugar over the top.

Bake for 20–25 minutes, turning the pan after about 12 minutes. The muffins are done when the tops look cracked, and when a toothpick inserted into the centre of one of the muffins comes out clean.

Let the muffins cool in the tin for about 5 minutes, then transfer them to a wire rack. Best served while warm.

Savoury muffins

Omit the spices and add a teaspoon of salt; replace the fruit with grated raw vegetables (courgettes, carrots or beetroot); add some chopped herbs and a couple of tablespoons of grated Cheddar or crumbled feta cheese.

Almond Croissants

· ·

These are a fun way to use up any leftover plain croissants – you might even find yourself buying croissants especially to make these almond versions. They can be assembled the night before and kept in the fridge ready to be baked the next morning. You can add cinnamon, bay leaves or cardamom to the syrup, but strain it before using.

80g sugar
100ml water
80g flaked almonds
50g salted butter, diced, at
   room temperature
1 egg, beaten, at room
   temperature
4 large day-old croissants,
   sliced in half horizontally
Icing sugar, for dusting

Put half the sugar with the water in a pan over a medium heat and boil for 1 minute, until the sugar has dissolved. Remove from the heat and leave to one side.

Preheat the oven to 180°C (170°C fan) and line a baking tray with baking parchment.

Use a food processor or a mortar and pestle to blend or crush the remaining sugar with 50g of the almonds until you have a coarse powder. Add the butter and beat until completely combined, then gradually add the egg and beat until creamy.

Brush each croissant inside and out with the sugar syrup – the croissants should be quite moist and sticky.

Spread the inside of each croissant with about 2 tablespoons of the almond mixture, then close and spread another 1 tablespoon of the mixture on the top. Repeat with the remaining croissants, and then sprinkle with the rest of the flaked almonds. (At this point, they can be kept in the fridge until ready to cook.)

Bake for 12–15 minutes, until the almond mixture has set and turned golden. Transfer to a wire rack, dust with icing sugar and serve slightly warm or at room temperature.

Bacon and Egg Bread Tartlets

Good bread never should go to waste. Use it for French Toast (see page 15) or the Savoury Bread and Butter Bake (see page 58), or whizz in the food processor to make your own breadcrumbs (endlessly useful). For this recipe the bread shouldn't be too stale as it must be pliable enough to press into the moulds. These would also be good to take on a picnic.

MAKES 12 TARTS

About 80g butter, softened, plus extra for greasing
12 thin slices of bread, crusts removed
6 slices of rindless streaky bacon, finely chopped
6 eggs
200ml whole milk
Salt and freshly ground black pepper
6 tbsp sweetcorn, fresh, tinned or frozen (optional)
200g Cheddar cheese, grated

Preheat the oven to 190°C (180°C fan) and grease a 12-hole muffin tin with butter.

Lightly butter both sides of the bread and push into the muffin tin, pressing right into the corners so the bread forms tart cases.

Divide the bacon equally among the bread-lined muffin tins and bake for 10–12 minutes, until the bread is crisp and starting to brown at the edges, and the bacon is cooked.

Whisk the eggs with the milk and season with salt and pepper (going easy on the salt because the cheese and bacon will be salty).

Remove the bread 'tarts' from the oven and divide the sweetcorn (if using) and cheese among the tarts. Pour in the egg mix and bake for 15 minutes, until the filling puffs up and the surface browns slightly. Don't worry if some of the egg mix spills over.

Leave to cool slightly – they are best served warm or at room temperature.

Baked Stuffed Mushrooms

Mushrooms made more glorious with a stuffing of leeks, herbs and breadcrumbs and a creamy mustard sauce. Serve with eggs as an epic brunch dish or, if you're up for the challenge, use smaller mushrooms for the fanciest mushrooms ever to grace your breakfast fry-up. Smaller stuffed mushrooms would also make brilliant canapés to serve with drinks.

4 tbsp butter

1 leek, finely sliced

1 onion, finely chopped

2 tsp chopped fresh thyme

8 slices of rindless streaky bacon, finely chopped (optional)

80g fresh white breadcrumbs

Small bunch of flat-leaf parsley, finely chopped

Salt and freshly ground black pepper

4 large field or Portobello mushrooms

1–2 tbsp Dijon mustard (to taste)

150ml double cream

4 eggs (optional)

Preheat the oven to 200°C (190°C fan).

Heat half the butter in a pan and cook the leek, half the onion, the thyme and the bacon (if using) for about 10 minutes until soft. Remove from the heat, stir in the breadcrumbs and half the parsley and season with salt and pepper.

Heat 1 tablespoon of the butter in a large frying pan and fry the mushrooms for a couple of minutes on each side, adding a pinch of salt as they cook.

Place the mushrooms on a baking tray and divide the leek and breadcrumb mix among the mushrooms, flattening with the back of a spoon. Bake for about 10 minutes, or until the filling is golden.

Meanwhile, fry the remaining onion in the remaining 1 tablespoon of butter for 5 minutes, until soft. Add the mustard and cream and bring to the boil to thicken, then season to taste, adding more mustard if you like.

Meanwhile, poach or fry the eggs (if using) and drain on kitchen paper.

When the mushrooms are cooked, top each with an egg, spoon over the cream sauce and serve immediately.

Croque Tartiflette

Tartiflette is the happiest of combinations: potatoes and ham, draped with cheese and baked until bubbling. It is the sort of dish best served on a cold day and eaten with gusto. This version is a hybrid with that brunch favourite Croque Monsieur, and is built for a heavy-duty brunch offering. Serve with a green salad, dressed simply and sharply with a little red wine vinegar, olive oil and salt and pepper, and some tiny cornichons, gherkins or pickled onions.

2 tbsp butter
2 tbsp plain flour
300ml whole milk, warmed
Salt and freshly ground
    black pepper
2 egg yolks
120g waxy potatoes, boiled in
    salted water until tender,
    then thinly sliced
1 shallot, very finely chopped
    (optional)
4 thick slices of sourdough
    or ciabatta bread
4 slices of smoked ham
    (cured or cooked)
200g cheese (Gruyère,
    reblochon, raclette or
    Taleggio), sliced or grated

Melt the butter in a saucepan and add the flour. Mix well and cook for about 2 minutes until it starts to bubble slightly. Whisk in the milk, a little at a time, until fully incorporated, bring to the boil, then turn down the heat and cook for 5 minutes, until thickened and smooth. Season with salt and pepper, remove from the heat and beat in the egg yolks.

Preheat the oven to 200°C (190°C fan) or preheat the grill.

Toss the cooked potatoes and the shallot (if using) with the white sauce and add salt and pepper to taste.

Toast the bread lightly. Spread a quarter of the potato and sauce mix on to each slice of toast, and top with the ham and the cheese.

Place on a baking sheet and bake or grill until the cheese is golden and bubbling and it is hot throughout, about 5–10 minutes.

Serve immediately, perhaps with mustard and some cornichons, certainly with napkins.

Chorizo Hash Brown

Hash browns are a boon for any fry-up, and these chorizo versions are turbocharged! You can serve these solo, with no other sidekicks, though a fried egg and some tomatoes are very good. You could make individual hash browns, but I like to make one large version, slicing it into large wedges.

3 tbsp olive oil
1 onion, finely chopped
½ bunch of spring onions, finely sliced
2 garlic cloves, finely chopped
800g waxy potatoes, peeled
100g chorizo (hot or mild), casing removed, finely chopped
Small bunch of flat-leaf parsley, roughly chopped
Salt and freshly ground black pepper
4 eggs, to serve (optional)
Roasted or fried tomatoes, to serve (optional)
Hot or sweet paprika, to serve

Heat 1 tablespoon of the oil in a large frying pan and fry the onion until soft, about 5 minutes. Add the spring onions and garlic and fry for 2 minutes. Transfer to a large bowl and keep the pan to one side – no need to clean it at this stage.

Coarsely grate the potatoes, then gather them in a clean tea towel and squeeze out as much liquid as possible. Mix the potatoes into the onion mix along with the chorizo, parsley and some salt and pepper.

Heat the remaining oil in the pan over a medium heat, then add the potato mixture and press down with a spatula. Cook for about 10 minutes, or until browned on the bottom.

Place a plate on top of the pan and carefully flip so the potato mixture is on the plate.

Slide the potatoes back into the pan, cooked-side up, and cook for another 7–8 minutes, until cooked through and browned on both sides.

Meanwhile, fry the eggs and/or tomatoes (if using).

Slide the hash on to a chopping board. Dust with a little paprika, then cut into wedges and serve.

Spiced Chicken and Avocado Sandwich

This is inspired by Antipodean café culture, where brunch rules supreme and sandwiches are full to bursting with wholesome ingredients and big, fresh flavours. I've suggested using a Cajun or piri piri spice blend here, but you can by all means use your own favourite spice blend. Good-quality bread will make a difference here – think doorstop!

4 skinless chicken breasts, or boneless skinless thighs
2 tbsp olive oil
About 2 tbsp Cajun or piri piri spice blend
1 garlic clove, crushed
4 tbsp mayonnaise
1 lemon or lime
Salt and freshly ground black pepper
2 ripe avocados, peeled and stoned
4 crusty bread rolls or ciabatta rolls, halved
4 slices of Cheddar cheese (optional)
2 tomatoes, thinly sliced
1 soft green lettuce, washed and dried

Rub the chicken with the olive oil, then roll in the spice mix to coat evenly.

Mix the garlic into the mayonnaise with a squeeze of lemon or lime juice, and check the seasoning, adding salt and pepper to taste.

Preheat the grill.

Fry or grill the chicken for about 5 minutes on each side, until charred on the outside and just done in the middle. Add a squeeze of lemon or lime juice, cover with foil and leave to rest in a warm place for a couple of minutes while you prepare the rest of the sandwich.

Mash the avocados and season to taste with salt, pepper and a squeeze of lemon or lime juice.

Toast the halved rolls under the grill, then place a slice of cheese (if using) on the bottom half of each roll and grill until melted. Spread the top half with the mayonnaise.

Thinly slice the chicken, check the seasoning and place on top of the cheese. Top with tomato, avocado and lettuce leaves and serve immediately.

Hot-Smoked Salmon, Watercress and Mustard Butter on Brown Bread

Hot-smoked salmon is an endlessly versatile ingredient. On toast, in a salad or scrambled into eggs, hot-smoked salmon can save many an emergency breakfast, brunch, lunch or dinner. With watercress and mustard, the combination is a classic. Store any excess mustard butter in the fridge – perfect for ham sandwiches or to top grilled meats or roasted vegetables. Salting and rinsing onions will soften their flavour and texture, giving the onion slices an almost-cooked appearance.

½ small red onion, very thinly sliced

Salt and freshly ground black pepper

80g butter, softened

2 tsp Dijon mustard

2 tsp wholegrain mustard (or use just one type of mustard)

Finely grated zest and juice of ½ lemon

1 ripe avocado, peeled and stoned

150–200g hot-smoked salmon fillets, broken into chunks

4 thick slices of brown grainy bread

Bunch of watercress, washed and dried, roughly chopped (optional)

Preheat the oven to 200°C (190°C fan).

Rub a large pinch of salt into the onion for 1 minute, then rinse and drain well.

Beat the butter with the two mustards, the lemon zest and salt and pepper to taste.

Mash the avocado with the lemon juice and season to taste with salt and pepper.

Place the hot-smoked salmon on a baking tray and place in the oven for 5–10 minutes, until heated through. Break into large flakes.

Toast the bread and spread with the mustard butter, then with the avocado. Top with the salmon, a few onion slices and some watercress.

Cheddar and Bacon Cornbread Muffins

....

Cornbread goes down very well with various brunch offerings. Serve these muffins with some smoky paprika baked beans, bacon, creamy mushrooms or fried garlicky prawns. They are best eaten on the day they are made. In the unlikely event of any leftovers, crumble them and use instead of breadcrumbs in the stuffed mushroom recipe on page 39. Paper muffin cases are a good idea here as the batter may stick; alternatively, liberally grease the muffin tin with butter.

at the oven to 200°C (190°C fan). If not using paper n cases, grease a 12-hole muffin tin generously with butter ust with flour.

le bacon in the butter until starting to brown, then add nion and cook until soft, about 10 minutes.

rge mixing bowl, combine the flour, polenta and onate of soda with ½ teaspoon of salt, a good grind of pepper and the chilli flakes, and make a well in the centre.

g or bowl, beat the milk, sour cream and egg together, ix in the bacon, onion and all of the fat. Pour into the gredients along with the cheese and stir gently until just ned, but don't overmix.

into the muffin tin and bake for about 12–15 minutes a toothpick inserted into the centre of one of the comes out clean.

le muffins out on to a wire rack to cool slightly; these served warm.

Kipper Kedgeree

Kippers are a classic breakfast and brunch dish, served with a pile of hot buttered toast and a wedge of lemon. This quintessentially British smoked fish contains healthy proteins and omega-3 fats. Herrings, which are known as kippers when smoked, are one of the more sustainable fish supplies, as they are often caught in large shoals with little in the way of bycatch.

2 whole kippers
40g butter
1 large onion, finely chopped
250g young spinach leaves, or watercress
2 tsp mild (or hot) curry powder
½ tsp turmeric
300g white basmati rice, rinsed and drained
500ml vegetable or fish stock, or water
Salt and freshly ground black pepper
1 lemon: ½ for juice, the rest cut into wedges
4 soft-boiled eggs, peeled and halved
Small bunch of parsley, roughly chopped
Fresh green chilli, finely sliced (optional)

Put the kippers in a bowl or pan, cover with boiling water and leave for 10 minutes. Drain, then flake the flesh, discarding the skin and any bones.

Heat 30g of the butter in a large saucepan and fry the onion for 10 minutes, or until soft.

Add the curry powder and turmeric to the onion and cook for 30 seconds, then stir in the rice. Add the stock or water, reduce the heat to low and cover. Cook for about 14 minutes or until the rice is tender. Do not stir at all.

Meanwhile, in another pan, wilt the spinach or watercress with the rest of the butter, then drain and put to one side.

When the rice is cooked, stir through the cooked spinach or watercress, fluffing the rice as you go, then stir through the fish. Season to taste with salt, pepper and lemon juice.

Serve in bowls, topped with an egg and sprinkled with parsley and green chilli (if using), with a lemon wedge on the side.

LONG LUNCHES

This set of recipes represents the very best of weekend cooking. Even when the weather might look a little glum, turn your radio up, stick the kettle on and cook a proper lunch for all to enjoy. This is the time to tackle some pastry, or maybe experiment with some bold new flavours or one-pot wonders. Bright, confident cooking here – and singing along to the radio is pretty much obligatory.

Fried Fish Tacos

Tacos will always go down well. It's the best sort of meal, with everyone at the table assembling their own tacos, some adding more chilli, others preferring more lime and coriander. Panko are Japanese breadcrumbs and they give a fantastic crunch to fried foods. They are available in most supermarkets, but if you can't track them down you can use normal breadcrumbs. Chilli sauce will work here, but I like the kick of chopped fresh chilli.

100g mayonnaise or
    sour cream
Finely grated zest and juice
    of 2 limes
Salt and freshly ground
    black pepper
100g plain flour
2 tsp paprika
500g firm white fish fillet,
    cut into 10cm x 3cm
    strips
2 eggs, beaten and seasoned
    with a pinch of salt
300g panko (Japanese
    breadcrumbs), or other
    dry breadcrumbs
1 red onion, very thinly sliced
    (or Quick Pickled Red
    Onions, opposite)
150g white cabbage, very
    thinly sliced or shredded
Vegetable oil for frying
8 corn or wheat tortillas,
    warmed
Small bunch of coriander,
    roughly chopped
Fresh or pickled chillies,
    finely sliced, or chilli sauce

In a bowl, whisk the mayonnaise or sour cream with the zest and juice of 1 lime and add salt and pepper to taste. Put to one side.

Line a tray with baking parchment.

In a large plastic bag, combine the flour, paprika, 1 teaspoon salt and 1 teaspoon pepper. Add the fish, close the bag and shake to coat. Shaking off excess flour, put the fish pieces on a plate.

Put the eggs in a shallow dish and the breadcrumbs in another. Dip the fish in the egg and then in the breadcrumbs to coat all over, then place the pieces – spaced apart – on the lined tray.

Rub a large pinch of salt into the onion for 1 minute, then rinse and drain well and squeeze over the juice of ½ a lime.

Season the cabbage with the remaining lime juice and salt and pepper to taste.

Pour about 4cm of oil into a large, deep pan and carefully heat to 180°C, or until a piece of onion or cube of bread begins to sizzle immediately and brown within 20 seconds.

Fry the fish in batches until golden all over, about 2 minutes on each side. Remove with a slotted spoon and drain the fish on kitchen paper.

Serve the fish in the tortillas with the lime mayonnaise, the cabbage and the red onion. Top with coriander, adding chilli to taste.

Quick Pickled Red Onions

2 small red onions, thinly
 sliced
200ml white wine or cider
 vinegar
1 garlic clove, halved
1 tsp sugar
½ tsp salt
1 small dried chilli or ½ tsp
 chilli flakes (optional)

Put the onions in a bowl, pour boiling water over them and
leave for 30 seconds, then drain in a sieve over the sink.

Put the vinegar, garlic, sugar, salt and chilli (if using) in a small
pan and bring to the boil until the salt and sugar have dissolved.

Put the onions in a jar, pour over the vinegar and stir or
shake gently.

The onions will be ready in about 30 minutes, but are better
after a few hours. Store in the fridge for up to a week.

Moroccan Spiced Chicken Pie

This is a real showstopper. The cooked pie, or to give it its Moroccan name, pastilla, is dusted with icing sugar and cinnamon and brought to the table. It is an intoxicating moment when the crisp pastry is cut into and the steamy, spicy aroma escapes. Use a medley of roasted root vegetables (carrots, beetroot, parsnips) instead of the chicken if you prefer, adding them at the same time as the eggs. Serve with harissa or chilli sauce and a great big green salad.

1 tbsp olive oil

700g boneless chicken thighs

80g butter, melted

2 onions, finely chopped

3 garlic cloves, finely chopped

1 tsp ground cinnamon

1 tsp ground ginger

Seeds from 6 cardamom pods, crushed

½ tsp turmeric

Pinch of saffron (optional)

300ml chicken or vegetable stock, or water

Salt and freshly ground black pepper

75g dried dates, apricots or raisins, roughly chopped

75g almonds or pistachios, chopped

1 tbsp honey

3 eggs, beaten

Small bunch of parsley or coriander, finely chopped

5 large sheets of filo pastry

1 tbsp icing sugar

Harissa, to serve (optional)

Heat the olive oil in a large frying pan and fry the chicken for about 8 minutes, or until browned all over. Put to one side on a plate.

Add 1 tablespoon of the melted butter to the pan, add the onions and cook for 10 minutes until soft. Add the garlic, half the cinnamon and the rest of the spices and cook for 1 minute more.

Return the chicken to the pan and add the stock. Season with salt and pepper and simmer for about 20 minutes or until the chicken is cooked through.

Remove the chicken and set it aside to cool slightly. Boil the liquid in the pan to reduce to about 100ml.

Roughly chop the chicken and return to the pan along with the dried fruit, nuts and honey. Add the eggs and cook gently until the mix resembles loose scrambled eggs, then add the herbs and put to one side.

Preheat the oven to 180°C (170°C fan). You will need a baking dish large enough to hold the chicken mix (about 25 x 20cm should do it). Brush the dish with melted butter.

Take a sheet of filo pastry and brush it with melted butter. Drape it over the baking dish, gently pushing it into the corners. Repeat with another sheet of filo, placing it at a right angle to the first. Repeat with two more sheets of filo to form a pastry case.

Spoon the chicken mixture into a round heap in the centre of the pastry, and then fold the pastry sides over the meat to make

a pie. Lay the remaining sheet of filo on top, brush with butter and tuck under any corners.

Bake for about 30 minutes, until the pastry is crisp and golden brown. Remove from the oven and leave to cool a little before dusting it with the icing sugar and the rest of the cinnamon.

Baked Giant Meatballs

Shout 'meatballs' and my bet is everyone will want to dash to the table with napkins at the ready! Giant meatballs will certainly raise a few eyebrows – mention they're stuffed, and your guests will be bowled over. Serve with a green salad with plenty of chopped fresh mint, or with a diced cucumber and red onion salad dressed with lemon juice. These meatballs are also knockout stuffed in a roll with lots of lettuce and a dollop of yogurt.

600g minced lamb or beef

1 onion, coarsely grated

3 tbsp breadcrumbs (or use plain flour)

1 egg, beaten

1 tsp ground turmeric

1 tsp ground coriander

½ tsp ground cinnamon, cardamom or nutmeg (optional)

Small bunch of flat-leaf parsley, finely chopped

Salt and freshly ground black pepper

50g dried cranberries or sour cherries

50g pine nuts or chopped almonds

40g butter

2 tbsp olive or vegetable oil

2 garlic cloves, crushed

400g tomato passata or tinned chopped tomatoes

150g plain yogurt, seasoned with salt, to serve

Flatbreads, to serve

Preheat the oven to 200°C (190°C fan).

In a large mixing bowl, mix the meat with half the onion, the breadcrumbs, egg, all the spices, the parsley, 1 teaspoon of salt and a good grind of pepper, and knead until evenly combined.

Divide the mix into four equal pieces and roll into balls. Stick your thumb deep into each ball to make a pocket, and then fill with the dried fruit and nuts and a little knob of butter. Close the meat mix over the filling.

Oil a large casserole dish or roasting tray, add the meatballs and drizzle with 2 tablespoons of oil, then roast in the oven for 20–25 minutes, until golden and sizzling.

Meanwhile, heat 2 tablespoons of butter in a pan and fry the remaining onion and the garlic for 5 minutes, until soft. Add the tomato and salt and pepper to taste and cook until thick and rich, about 10 minutes.

When the meatballs are cooked through, take the tray out of the oven and pour the tomato sauce over the meatballs, then return them to the oven for a couple of minutes.

Serve with seasoned yogurt drizzled over and flatbreads on the side.

Savoury Bread and Butter Bake

Bread and butter pudding, savoury style. This recipe makes brilliant use of slightly stale bread. It can be served as a side dish for a big lunch to feed many, or serve it just as it is with a green salad or some cooked green beans on the side. Leave out the ham if you like, and by all means add some fried mushrooms or cooked cubed sweet potato for extra vegetable oomph.

2 leeks, thickly sliced

1 head broccoli, broken into florets (about 200g total)

100g mature Cheddar or Lancashire cheese, grated

100g chopped cooked ham (optional)

200g sliced white bread (such as sourdough), crusts left on

50g butter, softened

2 tsp Dijon mustard

300ml whole milk

3 eggs, beaten

Pinch of grated nutmeg

Salt and freshly ground black pepper

Small bunch each of parsley and marjoram or thyme, roughly chopped

Preheat the oven to 180°C (170°C fan).

Boil the leeks and broccoli together in salted water for 5 minutes, or until tender, then drain well. Place in a baking dish and top with half the cheese and all of the ham (if using).

Spread the bread generously with the butter and mustard, then lay on top of the vegetables, buttered-side up.

Whisk together the milk, eggs, nutmeg and plenty of salt and pepper. Stir in the herbs, then gently pour over the bread. Scatter the remaining cheese on top and leave to soak for 10 minutes.

Bake for 35–45 minutes, or until puffed up, golden brown and just set in the centre. Serve immediately.

Lancashire Hotpot

An undisputed classic, this will always make for a really special lunch. The top potato layer, bronzed and crisp in places, looks especially impressive when brought to the table. You can add a bit of raw lamb liver and kidney in the mix if you enjoy eating offal. If you come across mutton or hogget (from a sheep older than one year), do give this a go as the flavour will be deeper, just be aware the cooking time might be a little longer for the meat to be melting and soft. Pickled red cabbage, which you can buy or make, is the traditional accompaniment, and to be honest, nothing really beats it.

6 slices of lamb or mutton neck with bone (or use lamb or mutton chops)

300g diced lamb or mutton neck fillet or shoulder

4 tbsp plain or wholemeal flour

Salt and freshly ground black pepper

3 large potatoes (about 800g), such as Maris Piper, peeled and thinly sliced

2 onions, thinly sliced

1 sprig of thyme, finely chopped

3 tbsp butter

2 bay leaves

500ml lamb or chicken stock, or water

Preheat the oven to 180°C (170°C fan), and dust all the meat with flour, salt and pepper.

Toss the potatoes, onions and thyme together and season with salt and pepper.

Grease a deep casserole dish with 1 tablespoon of the butter and arrange one-third of the potato and onion mix in the bottom. Top with the meat and bay leaves.

Add the remaining potato mix, overlapping the top layer of slices attractively. Pour in enough stock to come up to the topping (the stock should be just visible).

Melt the remaining butter and pour over the top. Cover and bake for about 2 hours (a bit longer for mutton, until it feels tender when prodded with a skewer).

Uncover the casserole and bake for about 20 minutes, until the potatoes on top are golden brown and crisp. Leave to rest for 10 minutes before serving; remove the bay leaves as you serve.

Flamiche (Flemish Leek Tart)

Flamiche is a recipe from northern France that uses yeasted dough. Flamiche sets the humble leek centre stage and, as such, it is important to cook the leeks until they are very soft, as this will make them all the sweeter and tastier. You can add a couple of rashers of bacon or sliced ham to the leek mix, but I rarely bother.

175g plain flour, plus extra
    for rolling
½ tsp dried yeast
¼ tsp salt
110ml warm water
Salt and freshly ground
    black pepper
3 tbsp olive oil
30g butter
500g leeks, white part only,
    sliced thinly
2 eggs
150g sour cream or crème
    fraîche
1 tsp chopped fresh thyme
Freshly grated nutmeg
20g Parmesan or Cheddar
    cheese, grated

Make the dough as for the empanada recipe on page 63; this time you will need only ¼ teaspoon of salt, 1 tablespoon of olive oil, and 110ml water.

While the dough is proving, prepare the topping: heat the butter in a frying pan and cook the leeks in 2 tablespoons of olive oil for 10 minutes, until really soft and sweet. Leave to cool a little.

Beat the eggs in a bowl. Add the cream, thyme, salt, pepper and plenty of nutmeg to taste. Add the slightly cooled leeks.

Preheat the oven to 200°C (190°C fan). Line a baking tray (approx. 40 x 30cm) with greaseproof paper and grease with the remaining 1 tablespoon of oil.

Lightly flour the work surface and roll out the dough to fit the baking tray: it should be about 5mm thick. Make a small lip around the edge of the dough and spoon the leek mixture on top, spreading it out evenly. Sprinkle the cheese over the leeks.

Bake for 20–25 minutes until the top is nicely coloured and the base is crisp. Remove from the oven and serve immediately, although it is still delicious served warm or cold.

Tuna and Pepper Empanada

Empanadas make an impressive, albeit fairly effortless, lunch offering. This recipe is based on Galician empanadas, from the north-west of Spain. It is made with yeasted dough and I've made it as one large pie rather than individual pasties.

350g plain flour, plus extra
   for rolling
1 tsp dried yeast
Salt and freshly ground
   black pepper
225ml warm water
100ml extra virgin olive oil
2 green peppers, deseeded
   and roughly chopped
3 onions, finely chopped
10 garlic cloves, thinly sliced
1 tsp paprika (sweet, hot or
   smoked)
400g tin whole tomatoes,
   well drained (use the juice
   for something else)
2 x 250g cans bonito tuna,
   or other sustainable tuna,
   in oil, drained
2 hard-boiled eggs, peeled
   and roughly chopped
1 egg, beaten

In a bowl, mix together the flour, yeast and ½ teaspoon of salt. Add the warm water and 2 tablespoons of the olive oil and mix until fully incorporated. Cover and put to one side for 10 minutes. Knead the dough for a couple of minutes, then form into a ball by tucking the dough under itself. Transfer to an oiled bowl, cover with clingfilm and set aside in a warm place until just about doubled in size, about 1 hour.

Meanwhile, make the filling: heat 3 tablespoons of the oil in a pan and fry the peppers and onions for about 15 minutes, until very soft and sweet. Add the garlic and paprika and cook for 4 minutes until the garlic is soft. Add the tomatoes and cook until thickened and any liquid has evaporated. Stir in the tuna and the hard-boiled eggs and season with salt and pepper to taste.

Preheat the oven to 180°C (170°C fan). Line a baking tray (approx. 40 x 30cm) with greaseproof paper and grease generously with the remaining olive oil. Divide the dough in half and shape into two balls. On a lightly floured work surface, roll out the first ball until it is slightly larger than the baking tray. Place the dough on the baking tray. Spoon the filling on to the dough and smooth it into an even layer.

Roll out the second ball of dough until it is the same size as the tray and place on top of the filling. Cut off any pastry that hangs over the sides. Seal the sides of the empanada by pressing and rolling the top and bottom layers of dough together. Cut a small hole in the centre of the dough to allow steam to vent. Brush with the beaten egg. Bake until browned on top and piping hot throughout, 45–55 minutes. Remove from the oven and leave to cool slightly. Cut into pieces and serve at room temperature.

Chicken and Leek Pie

It's pretty tricky to beat a pie for lunch! Pies are also a fantastic way to use up leftover roast chicken. I've used spelt flour for the pastry here: spelt is an ancient grain with a nutty, wholesome flavour which has gained in popularity in recent years. Use plain or wholemeal flour if you can't find spelt flour or would prefer to stick with your usual pastry combination.

175g very cold butter, cut into very small cubes

300g spelt flour, plus 2 tbsp for the sauce and extra for rolling

Salt and freshly ground black pepper

200g leeks, sliced

300g chestnut or button mushrooms

250ml chicken stock

300ml double cream

600g cooked (roast or poached) chicken, skinned and roughly chopped

2 tsp roughly chopped tarragon leaves

2 tbsp Dijon mustard

1 egg, beaten

Rub 150g of the butter into the flour and ½ teaspoon of salt, using your fingertips or a food processor, until it resembles breadcrumbs. Add about 3 tablespoons of very cold water until the dough just comes together, then knead very gently until just incorporated. Try to not over-knead the dough.

Shape the dough into a flattened disc, wrap in clingfilm and put in the fridge while you make the filling.

Preheat the oven to 200°C (190°C fan).

Heat the remaining 25g of butter in a pan and fry the leeks for 5 minutes until soft. Add the mushrooms and ½ teaspoon of salt and cook for 2 minutes. Add 2 tablespoons of flour and cook for 1 minute.

Add the chicken stock and cream, bring to the boil, then boil to reduce the liquid until thick enough to coat the back of a spoon.

Add the cooked chicken, tarragon and mustard. Season with salt and pepper to taste, then pour into a pie dish.

On a lightly floured surface, roll out the pastry to about 1cm thick, rolling in one direction only. Cut out the pastry to a little larger than your pie dish, and then lay it on top. Using a sharp knife, cut around the side of the dish to trim excess pastry and then crimp the pastry around the edges to seal the dish. Cut a small hole in the centre of the pastry, then brush with the beaten egg.

Bake for 30 minutes, or until the pastry is golden brown and cooked. Serve immediately.

Boiled Ham and Parsley Sauce

This may appear to be a humble, frugal-sounding recipe, but, made with care and attention, it is anything but. Served with buttered boiled potatoes and a pot of mustard on the table, this is first-class comfort food. Add a big handful of watercress in lieu of the parsley if making this in the springtime. You want the sauce to be a vivid and arresting shade of green.

2 unsmoked ham hocks
2 large carrots, cut
    into chunks
3 celery stalks, roughly
    chopped
2 large onions: 1½ quartered,
    ½ finely chopped
2 tsp black peppercorns
2 bay leaves
400ml whole milk
Large bunch of curly parsley,
    stalks separated, leaves
    very finely chopped
50g butter
50g plain flour
Salt and freshly
    ground black pepper
75ml double cream
Boiled potatoes and
    mustard, to serve

Soak the hocks in water for about 8 hours (overnight is good), changing the water a couple of times.

Put the hocks in a large pan, cover with cold water and bring to the boil. Skim any scum off the surface and add the carrots, celery, quartered onion, peppercorns and bay leaves and simmer gently for about 2–3 hours, until the meat is coming away from the bone.

Remove 200ml of the cooking liquid and put it in a saucepan with the milk, chopped onion and the parsley stalks. Bring to the boil, remove from the heat and leave to infuse for 15 minutes, then strain.

Heat the butter in a small saucepan, add the flour and cook for 1 minute, then start whisking in the infused milk, whisking until smooth before you add more. Simmer for 4 minutes, whisking all the time, then stir in the cream, followed by the parsley, and cook for a few minutes, adding salt and pepper to taste. Cover to keep warm.

Remove and discard the fat from the hocks and cut the meat into large chunks, then warm through in the remaining ham stock. Serve the ham with the parsley sauce, boiled potatoes and mustard.

Jambalaya

Jambalaya is a Creole and Cajun rice dish, with Spanish, African and French influences. There are many regional variations, but one thing that all jambalayas have in common is the 'holy trinity' of Cajun and Creole cookery: onion, celery and green pepper are the backbone of this flavoursome, one-pot recipe.

500g boneless
    chicken thighs
1 tsp hot smoked paprika
1 tsp ground cumin
½ tsp ground coriander
Salt and freshly ground
    black pepper
3 tbsp olive or vegetable oil
1 small chorizo ring (about
    200g) or smoked Polish
    sausage, cut into bite-
    sized pieces
1 onion, finely chopped
3 celery stalks, finely
    chopped
1 green pepper, deseeded
    and finely chopped
1 red pepper, deseeded
    and finely chopped
2 garlic cloves, crushed
1 tsp paprika (sweet or hot)
1 tsp chopped fresh thyme
1 tsp dried oregano
400g tin whole plum
    tomatoes, drained (use the
    juice for something else)
250g long-grain rice (not
    the easy-cook type)
500ml chicken stock
200g large raw prawns
Tabasco or hot sauce,
    to serve

Preheat the oven to 180°C (170°C fan).

Mix the chicken with the smoked paprika, cumin, coriander, salt and pepper. This can be done up to 8 hours ahead, covered and stored in the fridge.

Heat the oil in a large ovenproof pan and fry the chicken and chorizo for about 8 minutes until the chicken is lightly browned all over.

Using a slotted spoon, remove the chicken and chorizo and set aside in a bowl, leaving the oil in the pan.

Add the onion, celery and peppers and fry for 10 minutes, until soft.

Add the garlic, paprika, thyme and oregano and cook for 1 minute, then add the tomatoes and cook over a high heat for 5 minutes until slightly thickened.

Add the rice, stir well and cook for around 2 minutes, until the rice begins to turn opaque.

Return the cooked chicken and chorizo, along with any juices remaining in the bowl. Add the stock and cook over a medium heat for 10 minutes.

Cover the pan with foil and place in the oven for 10 minutes, then add the prawns, cover again and cook for a further 5–10 minutes until the liquid is absorbed and the rice and prawns are cooked. Leave to rest for 5 minutes before serving with hot sauce.

Mussels with a Fennel and Saffron Broth

Picking over a huge bowl of aromatic steaming mussels is the epitome of a relaxing, convivial lunch. Mussels are at their seasonal best from September to April. I've added some cooked rice to the liquid here, as I love how the rice absorbs the flavoursome broth. Crusty bread is also essential to soak up the juices. Serve with a glass of chilled rosé or white wine.

2 tbsp extra virgin olive oil

200g finocchiona salami, chorizo or pancetta, finely chopped (optional)

1 small fennel bulb, finely chopped

1 small onion, finely chopped

3 garlic cloves, finely chopped

Salt and freshly ground black pepper

50ml pastis, Pernod or white wine (optional)

Pinch of saffron, soaked in 2 tbsp warm water

Pinch of chilli flakes or powder

1 strip of orange zest, white pith removed

3 ripe tomatoes, chopped (or use ½ a 400g tin whole plum tomatoes, drained)

1.5kg mussels, cleaned

Small bunch of flat-leaf parsley, finely chopped

Juice of ½ lemon

200g cooked rice (optional)

1 tbsp butter

Heat the olive oil in a large, deep saucepan and fry the salami (if using) for 1 minute until the fat begins to run out, then add the fennel, onion and garlic. Reduce the heat to medium, season with salt and pepper, and cook until soft, about 10 minutes.

Add the alcohol, saffron, chilli, orange zest and tomatoes, increase the heat and cook for 30 seconds.

Add the mussels, cover and cook, shaking the pan frequently, for about 5 minutes until the mussels are open (after 1 minute, peek every 30 seconds or so to keep an eye on the mussels opening: you don't want them to overcook). As soon as all the mussels are open, stir through the parsley and lemon juice.

Using a slotted spoon, transfer the mussels to a bowl and place the pan lid over the bowl to keep warm.

Add the rice and butter to the pan to warm through and check the seasoning, adding more salt, pepper, chilli or lemon juice to taste.

Return the mussels to the pan, stir to combine, then transfer to a warm serving bowl.

Cleaning mussels

If the mussels are sandy, gritty or have hairy beards coming out of their shells, rinse and scrub them well under cold water and pull out the beards by pulling them towards the hinge end of the mussel. Discard any cracked mussels and any mussels that won't close when tapped firmly against the side of a bowl.

Fennel and Taleggio Tart

The trick with pastry (and it's a quickly learned one) is to be confident enough to mix the dough so it's cohesive, but to not overwork it, otherwise it becomes leaden when cooked. Blind baking – cooking the pastry before adding the filling – makes for a super-crisp tart base. Taleggio cheese has an edible salty crust and soft middle, and pairs beautifully with fennel, but use a blue cheese here if you prefer. You will need a 24-cm tart tin.

300g shortcrust pastry (or use the recipe for Chicken and Leek Pie on page 64, using plain, wholemeal or spelt flour, or a mix)

2 fennel bulbs, finely sliced (fronds reserved and chopped if there are enough, or use parsley)

1 red onion, finely sliced

20g butter

Salt and coarsely ground black pepper

4 large eggs, beaten

250ml whole milk

200g Taleggio or blue cheese, chopped into little pieces or crumbled

1 tsp crushed fennel seeds

First, make the pastry case. Dust the rolling pin and work surface lightly with flour. Roll out the dough using short rolls in one direction only, turning the dough a few times to make a round shape. When the dough is about 5cm larger than the tart tin, lift it up by carefully rolling it around the rolling pin and lay it across the tart tin. Press the dough into the corners of the tin using your fingers, but don't trim it yet. Chill for 30 minutes.

Preheat the oven to 200°C (190°C fan).

Fill the pastry case with a disc of baking paper and add dried beans to weigh it down. Bake for 15 minutes, then carefully remove the paper with the beans (which can be used to bake blind again) and cook the pastry for another 5 minutes.

Carefully trim off the excess pastry using a small sharp knife.

Turn the oven down to 160°C (150°C fan).

While the pastry is being baked, cook the fennel and onion in the butter in a covered pan over low heat until meltingly soft, about 15 minutes. Don't allow the fennel to colour – keep the heat low and stir occasionally.

Remove the lid, turn up the heat and cook until all the moisture has evaporated from the fennel and onion. Stir in ½ teaspoon of pepper and season with salt to taste. Leave to cool a little.

Whisk the eggs and milk together until well combined, and season with salt and pepper.

Spread the cooked fennel and onion over the base of the blind-baked pastry and scatter over the cheese, then carefully pour the

egg mix over the cheese. Scatter over the fennel seeds, another
½ teaspoon of black pepper and the chopped fennel fronds and/
or parsley.

Bake until the custard in the centre is set, 20–25 minutes.
Remove from the oven and leave to cool in the tin for about 30
minutes before removing from the tin. Cut into wedges to serve.

Brown Rice Bowls

This recipe is loosely based on bibimbap, a Korean dish that translates as 'mixed rice'. Nowadays it might well be referred to as a rice bowl. There are no rules for bibimbap, a wholesome, pleasing meal that encourages the cook to use as much or as little as you have to hand in your fridge and store cupboard. A fried egg perched on top is simply stupendous.

4 fresh red chillies, deseeded and roughly chopped

2 roasted red peppers (from a jar, or roasted in a hot oven until soft, then deseeded and peeled)

1 garlic clove, chopped

1 tbsp rice, white wine or cider vinegar

1 tsp sugar

5 tbsp vegetable oil

Salt and freshly ground black pepper

300g short-grain brown rice (or use white rice if you prefer – follow packet instructions to cook)

1 pointed cabbage or small white cabbage

4 tbsp sunflower or sesame seeds

400g mushrooms, sliced or quartered

1 bunch of spring onions, cut into 3cm lengths

4 eggs

Small bunch of basil, coriander or mint, roughly chopped

Soy sauce, to serve

Sesame oil, to serve

Preheat the oven to 200°C (190°C fan).

Using a food processor or mortar and pestle, blend the chillies, roasted peppers, garlic, vinegar, sugar, 2 tablespoons of the oil and salt and pepper to taste until you have a coarse paste. Put to one side.

Boil the brown rice in twice its volume of cold water and a big pinch of salt for 20–25 minutes or until tender. Make sure it doesn't boil dry, adding a little more boiling water if needed.

Meanwhile, cut the cabbage into six thick wedges and toss in 1 tablespoon of the oil, some salt and pepper, then roast in the oven for around 20 minutes, until just cooked through and charred in places; it should still have a fair bit of crunch. Chop into thick slices.

Sprinkle the seeds on a baking sheet and toast them in the hot oven for 5 minutes until golden, then put to one side.

Heat 2 tablespoons of the oil in a frying pan over a high heat and fry the mushrooms until they are starting to brown at the edges, then season with salt and pepper to taste. Remove from the pan and put to one side.

Fry the spring onions in the same pan as the mushrooms until just starting to brown. Put to one side.

Fry the eggs in the same pan as the spring onions.

Drain the rice and spoon into bowls then top with the cabbage, spring onions, mushrooms and egg, then top the lot with the seeds and herbs. Serve the chilli paste, soy sauce and sesame oil on the side to stir through the rice.

ROASTS

It's everyone's favourite meal, isn't it? Whether desert island dish or last supper, a roast dinner is the culinary showstopper we all love to eat. Which is why – especially if you love cooking as much as I do – it's essential that roast dinners don't become humdrum or boring. Same old, same old, pass the gravy? Never! Instead, choose one of these recipes to wow your family and friends and strike a canny balance between traditional, contemporary and downright delicious.

Roast Pork and Butter Beans

This is a simple take on a traditional Sunday lunch. One pan, Spanish style, with loads of butter beans spiked with paprika, garlic and tomatoes to soak up the roast pork juices. The skin should still get the characteristic roast pork crackle when you crank up the heat of the oven near the end of the cooking time. Use any cooked beans but, in this dish, I find the bigger the bean, the better.

SERVES ABOUT 6

1.5kg piece of boneless pork belly, skin scored in thin lines

Salt and freshly ground black pepper

2 onions, roughly chopped

3 carrots, roughly chopped

2 leeks, roughly chopped

6 garlic cloves, peeled and left whole

3 ripe tomatoes, roughly chopped, or drained plum tomatoes

2 tbsp extra virgin olive oil

100ml dry white wine (or use a light red wine)

1–2 tsp smoked paprika

2 tsp ground coriander

Large bunch of fresh thyme or rosemary, roughly chopped

2 x 400g tins butter beans (or use cooked white beans), drained and rinsed

Approx. 300ml stock or water

Preheat the oven to 220°C (200°C fan).

Season the pork belly all over with salt and pepper, rubbing it into the skin.

Mix the onions, carrots, leeks, garlic and tomatoes with the olive oil, wine, spices and herbs. Put to one side.

Roast the pork in a large, deep roasting tin for 30 minutes, until the skin is brown and bubbly. Take the pork out of the roasting tin and tip in the vegetable mix. Place the pork on top and cover tightly with foil.

Turn the oven down to 160°C (150°C fan) and cook for 1½ hours.

When the time is up, carefully remove the foil and add the beans and stock and stir through – it should be like a loose stew. Cover and return to the oven for about 30 minutes until the pork is easily pierced with a sharp knife.

Turn the oven up to 200°C (190°C fan) and remove the foil. Roast the pork for a further 15–30 minutes, or until the skin crackles, taking care the beans don't scorch.

Remove from the oven and leave to rest in a warm place for about 20 minutes. Check the seasoning of the vegetables and beans.

Transfer the cooked meat to a board and chop into thick slices; serve with the vegetables and beans.

Crying Leg of Lamb Boulangère

This French-inspired recipe is called 'crying' because the leg of lamb is slashed all over prior to cooking; its delicious juices 'weep' over the potatoes beneath as they cook in the oven. Boulangère is a French term for 'bakers' and references an era when many homes didn't own an oven and home cooks would take their prepared uncooked dishes to roast in the oven of their local bakery. Leftover meat from this roast makes a gorgeous sandwich.

SERVES 8

2kg leg of lamb, at room
    temperature
Salt and freshly ground
    black pepper
Small bunch of rosemary or
    thyme, finely chopped
2 tsp herbes de Provence
    (or another dried herb)
50ml olive oil
4 garlic cloves, sliced
800g waxy potatoes, peeled
    and thinly sliced
2 large onions, thinly sliced
400ml chicken or lamb
    stock, or water

Preheat the oven to 220°C (200°C fan).

Rub salt and pepper all over the leg. Mix the rosemary or thyme with the herbes de Provence and the olive oil.

Using a sharp pointed knife, stab about 20 deep slits all over the top of the leg. Rub the leg with about half of the herbed oil, pushing the herbs into the slits as much as you can, then push a slice of garlic into each slit. Place the meat in a deep roasting dish and put in the oven for 20 minutes to colour and develop a crust.

While the meat is cooking, toss the potatoes and onions together in a bowl and season with salt and pepper, adding the rest of the herbed oil and any leftover garlic.

After 20 minutes, take the meat out of the oven and put it on a large plate; turn down the oven to 180°C (170°C fan).

Tip the onion and potato mix into the roasting dish and pour over the stock, then put the lamb back on top. Return the roasting dish to the oven and roast for about 12–15 minutes per 500g if you want it pink, or 18 minutes per 500g if you want it well done.

When the meat is cooked, take it out of the oven and place on a carving board, wrap in foil and leave to rest for about 15 minutes.

Turn the oven temperature up to colour the potatoes a bit.

Carve the lamb and serve with the potatoes and onions.

Porchetta

Porchetta is the Italian equivalent of a hog roast – a slow roast joint of pork often stuffed into a soft roll and eaten outdoors, ideal for large gatherings. The larger the party, the bigger the joint – with a whole pig being the very best sort of spectacle. Boldly flavoured and studded with fennel, garlic and rosemary, this is a delicious riff on a Mediterranean classic.

SERVES 8

- 1.5kg piece of boneless pork belly, skin scored in thin lines
- Salt and freshly ground black pepper
- 250g plain pork sausages, skins removed (or use pork mince or sausage meat)
- 8 garlic cloves, crushed
- 2 tsp fennel seeds, toasted and crushed
- ½–1 tsp chilli flakes
- 2 tbsp chopped fresh rosemary
- 2 tbsp softened lard or olive oil
- Rolls, to serve

Place the pork belly skin-side down on a clean surface and slash the flesh about 1cm deep; season with salt and pepper.

Mix the sausage meat with the garlic, fennel seeds, chilli, rosemary and lard or oil, then smear the paste over the meat, pushing it into the slashes.

Roll up tightly and tie with butcher's string at about 5cm intervals. Place in the fridge, uncovered, for at least 1 hour, or overnight to marinate. Bring back to room temperature before cooking.

Preheat the oven to 160°C (150°C fan). Line a roasting tin with foil (this makes washing up a bit easier) and put a rack on the foil.

Pat the outside of the pork belly dry and put on the rack in the roasting tin. Rub salt into the cuts on the skin and roast for about 3–4 hours, until the pork is easily pierced with a sharp knife.

Turn the oven up to full heat and roast for a further 15–30 minutes or until the crackling is golden brown, making sure it doesn't scorch.

Remove from the oven and leave to rest, uncovered, for 30 minutes. You can make gravy at this point (see below).

Carve the pork into slices. Stuff into rolls and drizzle with sauce.

To make gravy

Remove the meat and rack from the roasting tin and leave to rest. Add 200ml wine or water to the roasting tin, stir to loosen the residue and then pour the whole lot into a pan over a medium heat. Boil until slightly thickened. Season to taste.

Persian Stuffed Lamb Shoulder

This is a beautifully aromatic roast that has an unctuously sweet filling of rice, dried fruit, nuts and spices. You could use this stuffing for a whole roast chicken or even a duck if you wanted to. As the meat cooks, the rice and dried fruit absorb the juices from the meat. A simple yogurt sauce is perfect to cut through the richness, as is a salad of diced cucumber and pomegranate seeds, with a bowl of steamed rice served on the side.

SERVES 6

30g butter
1 small carrot, finely chopped
2 small onions, finely
    chopped
100g basmati rice
Salt and freshly ground
    black pepper
½ tsp ground cinnamon
½ tsp ground green
    cardamom
1 tsp ground coriander
3 tbsp chopped almonds,
    walnuts, pine nuts or
    pistachios
3 tbsp dried cranberries,
    cherries or apricots,
    roughly chopped
Small pinch of saffron,
    infused in 3 tbsp hot
    water (or use 1 tsp
    turmeric)
Finely grated zest and juice
    of 1 orange
1.5kg boned shoulder of lamb
2 tbsp vegetable or olive oil
Yogurt, seasoned with salt
    and lemon juice, to serve

Heat the butter in a saucepan and cook the carrot and half the chopped onions for 5 minutes until soft. Add the rice and ½ teaspoon of salt and cook for 2 minutes, or until the rice begins to turn translucent.

Add the cinnamon, cardamom, coriander, nuts and dried fruit and stir to coat; cook for 1 minute, add 150ml of water, the saffron and soaking liquid, then cover and cook for 12 minutes, until the rice is just about cooked. Add the orange juice and zest and check the seasoning.

Preheat the oven to 220°C (200°C fan).

Place the shoulder skin-side down on a board and make about eight slashes in the meat to open it out as much as possible.

Press as much of the rice filling as will fit into the boned shoulder, then roll it up and tie with string and put into a roasting tin. Keep any leftover rice to one side. Rub the meat with the oil and season with salt and pepper; place in the oven for 35 minutes.

Turn the oven down to 180°C (170°C fan); add the rest of the onions and 200ml of water to the roasting tin, cover tightly with foil or a lid and roast for about 2 hours, or until cooked through and tender.

Uncover and add any remaining rice to the roasting tin; cook for a further 10 minutes to colour the meat and heat the rice, then remove from the oven, cover in foil and leave to rest for 10 minutes. Remove the string, slice the meat and serve with the yogurt sauce on the side.

Pot Roast Beef

This slow-cooked one-pot recipe is perfect to get on earlier in the day so you can head off out, safe in the knowledge that, when you return, you'll have a winning lunch on the table in about an hour. Do try to buy the best joint of meat your budget allows; when slow cooked the beef can dry out a bit if the cut is too lean or not aged well enough. Serve with mustard or horseradish on the side and a pile of greens.

SERVES 6

1.5kg piece of boneless beef chuck, shin or brisket

Salt and freshly ground black pepper

5 garlic cloves, crushed

2 tbsp chopped fresh thyme

3 tbsp melted dripping or vegetable oil

2 tbsp mustard (Dijon or English)

150ml beef stock, beer or water

1kg waxy potatoes, peeled and cut into bite-sized pieces

400g baby onions, peeled

2 carrots, cut into quarters

3 bay leaves

Small bunch of curly or flat-leaf parsley, finely chopped

Preheat the oven to 200°C (190°C fan).

Rub the meat with salt and pepper, then mix together the garlic, thyme, ½ teaspoon of salt, the oil and mustard and rub over the meat. Put the meat in a large roasting dish or casserole and place in the oven for 30 minutes to colour.

Turn the oven down to 140°C (130°C fan). Remove the roasting dish from the oven, add about 150ml beef stock, beer or water and cover the meat tightly with foil or a lid, then return to the oven for 3–4 hours or until very tender.

Add the potatoes, onions, carrots and bay leaves to the roasting dish and stir them into the juices along with a big pinch of salt and pepper. Turn the oven up to 160°C (150°C fan), cover the dish and return to the oven for 30 minutes until the vegetables are just cooked, then remove the foil or lid and return to the oven for 15 minutes to colour.

Leave to rest, covered, for about 15 minutes. Cut the meat into thick slices, stir the parsley through the sauce and serve the vegetables and any cooking juices with the meat.

Chicken with Forty Cloves of Garlic

Disarmingly simple; don't let the 40 cloves of garlic or the quantity of olive oil scare you off. If heaven is a perfect meal, then this might just be it. With just 10 minutes of prep time, this dish really couldn't be any easier. You will need a good heavy casserole pan with a tight-fitting lid to cook the bird. When the bird has finished cooking, reserve the leftover oil in the pan by skimming off the oil from the cooking juices and use this chicken-and-garlic-scented oil in any cooking over the next few days. I like potatoes with this – sautéed, boiled, roast or even mashed – and a green salad dressed simply with lemon juice, a pinch of salt and a drizzle of olive oil. Leftover chicken bones will make the best sort of chicken stock.

SERVES 4 GENEROUSLY

1 whole chicken (or 8 thighs if you prefer)
Salt and freshly ground black pepper
1 lemon, halved
Small bunch of fresh thyme
40 garlic cloves (about 3–4 heads), unpeeled
100ml extra virgin olive oil
200ml chicken stock or water
Small bunch of fresh herbs (parsley, tarragon or chives), finely chopped (optional)

Preheat the oven to 180°C (170°C fan).

Remove every bit of visible fat from the cavity of the chicken and season it inside and out with salt and pepper. Fill it with half the lemon and a couple of sprigs of thyme.

Place the chicken in the casserole with the garlic, olive oil and the rest of the thyme. Bring to a gentle simmer on the hob, then add the stock and cover tightly. Bake in the oven for about 1 hour (or about 45 minutes if you're using thighs), basting a couple of times and watching that the garlic doesn't get too brown before the chicken is cooked (if this happens, remove the garlic with a slotted spoon and put the pot back in the oven).

Leave the chicken to rest for 20 minutes, then squeeze over lemon juice to taste and scatter over the herbs (if using). I like to add a bit of extra black pepper too. Eat the garlic by squeezing the sweet flesh out on to the chicken.

Beef Wellington

This recipe is one for a really special weekend roast, although this has more to do with the cost of the ingredients rather than the level of difficulty. There are a few components to assemble, but, if you give yourself a bit of time and kitchen space, it's really rather straightforward. Placing the Wellington on to a hot baking sheet will help the bottom of the pastry to cook, although it's worth noting that the underside will always attract a bit of moisture from the cooking juices. I like to serve this with wilted or creamed spinach and not much else, to allow the meat and pastry to really take the limelight.

SERVES 4

15g dried porcini or shiitake
    mushrooms, soaked in hot
    water for 15 minutes
600g piece of beef fillet
Salt and freshly ground
    black pepper
1 tbsp beef dripping or
    vegetable oil
3 tbsp butter
3 shallots, finely chopped
350g mushrooms (chestnut,
    oyster or flat), finely
    chopped
2 tsp chopped fresh thyme
150ml Madeira
250g all-butter puff pastry
1 egg, beaten

Drain the soaked mushrooms and squeeze dry, then finely chop and put to one side.

Season the beef fillet all over with salt and fry in the dripping or vegetable oil in a very hot pan until well browned all over, taking care not to cook the meat too much. Remove and leave to cool on a plate.

Add the butter to the pan and fry the shallots until soft, about 5 minutes. Then add the mushrooms, chopped dried mushrooms, thyme and a big pinch of salt and cook until the mushrooms have released their liquid and the moisture has evaporated. Add the Madeira and cook until it has evaporated. Season with salt and pepper to taste. Spread the mushroom mixture on a plate and put to one side to cool.

Roll out the pastry to a rectangle about 25 x 30cm, with the short side closest to you.

Brush the pastry with half the egg and spread the mushroom mixture over. Put the beef at the end closest to you and carefully roll up.

Keep the pastry seam-side down, then fold the ends over and seal the pastry around the beef, cutting off any excess. You can decorate the pastry by scoring it if you want. Brush all over with egg and place on a piece of baking parchment; chill for about 15 minutes to let the pastry rest.

Preheat the oven to 200°C (190°C fan) and put a baking sheet in the oven.

When the oven is hot, lift the Wellington on its paper on to the hot baking sheet and cook for 30 minutes, until golden. Remove and leave to rest for 10 minutes, before slicing and serving with the side dishes of your choice. The beef should still be pink in the centre when you serve it.

Baked Whole Fish with Roasted Lemon, Potato and Dill

....

Roasting it on the bone is one of the easiest ways to cook fish – it also helps to keep moisture locked in the flesh of the fish. Cooking the fish together with the lemon and potatoes will give a bright, complex citrus flavour and wonderful cooking juices. I've used fresh dill and whole coriander seeds here to give a Greek flair to the recipe. Use parsley, oregano, thyme, marjoram or even sorrel if you prefer. To 'carve' the whole fish, carefully lift and remove the top fillet (removing any fin bones that you see), then peel away the bone in one go, starting at the tail end, leaving the bottom fillet on the plate or board.

SERVES 4

500g waxy small potatoes, washed but unpeeled

4 tbsp olive oil, plus extra to drizzle

Salt and freshly ground black pepper

1 tsp crushed fennel seeds

1 tsp crushed coriander seeds

½ a small glass dry white wine (or use water or fish stock)

1 unwaxed lemon

2 whole sea bream or bass (at least 600g each), gutted and scaled

Small bunch of dill, leaves roughly chopped, stalks kept

Preheat the oven to 200°C (190°C fan) and line a roasting tin with greaseproof paper.

Cut the potatoes into slices no thicker than a pound coin. Spread the potatoes evenly over the base of the lined roasting tin, coating them with half the olive oil, ½ teaspoon of salt, some pepper, the spices and the wine.

Cut the ends off the lemon about a quarter of the way from each end and put to one side to squeeze over later. Slice the middle of the lemon into four slices and lay on top of the potatoes, then cook in the oven for about 15 minutes.

Meanwhile, make three slits on each side of the fish. Season the fish inside and out with salt, pepper, half the dill and the remaining oil, putting the dill stalks into the belly of the fish.

Put the fish on top of the potatoes and cook for about 20 minutes, until the fish is cooked and the potatoes are soft and browned at the edges. To check that the fish is done, the flesh near the bone at the thickest part of the fish should be opaque and hot to touch, and you should just be able to pull the flesh from the bone.

Squeeze the juice from the reserved lemon ends over the fish and potatoes and add a drizzle of olive oil, then top with the rest of the chopped dill and serve immediately.

Duck with Prunes, Apples and Potatoes

A whole roasted duck with beautiful bronzed crisp skin is an impressive thing. With a large cavity, a duck is the perfect bird to stuff and roast – and, as the duck cooks, the fat will render and flavour the stuffing within. Here the apples and prunes swell with the cooking juices and duck fat. I like to serve this with some jarred sauerkraut warmed through in a little cream or fried in a little butter or some of the duck fat. Alternatively, serve with some steamed or boiled green or red cabbage. Leftover duck bones make terrific stock.

SERVES 4-6

1 whole duck (about 2kg)
Salt and freshly ground
    black pepper
1 tbsp cider vinegar, or use
    red or white wine vinegar
2 large eating apples,
    peeled, cored and roughly
    chopped
150g whole pitted prunes
Small bunch of fresh thyme,
    leaves picked
2 onions, quartered
500ml chicken stock, cider
    or water
700g potatoes, peeled and
    roughly chopped
2 tsp plain flour

Preheat the oven to 250°C – basically as high as your oven goes.

Remove the neck and giblets (and any other offal) from the duck cavity. Wipe the cavity and outside of the duck with kitchen paper and then rub both with salt and vinegar.

Mix the apples with the prunes, thyme, salt and pepper and stuff the duck as full as possible with the fruit mixture. Tie the thighs tightly up against the breast using kitchen string.

Place the bird, breast-side up, on a rack in a roasting tin containing the duck's neck and giblets and the onions, and roast for 20 minutes in the hot oven.

Remove the roasting tin from the oven and pour the cider or stock into the roasting tin. Turn the oven down to 150°C (140°C fan) and roast for another 1–1½ hours.

After about 1 hour, remove the duck from the oven, carefully spoon some of the fat into a bowl and return the duck to the oven. The duck is ready when the skin is golden and crisp and the meat is very tender.

Put the potatoes in a baking tray and toss in salt, pepper and the duck fat; put in the oven to roast until tender and browning at the edges.

When the duck is cooked, remove from the oven and leave to rest for 20 minutes. If the potatoes need a bit of colour, then crank the heat up now.

Strain the duck cooking juices from the roasting tin into a saucepan. Put the flour in a small bowl and whisk in about 100ml of the cooking juices, then add back into the saucepan, season with salt and pepper to taste, and cook for 5 minutes to thicken.

Chop the duck into eight pieces and serve with the apple and prune stuffing, the potatoes and the sauce.

Roast Chicken: Four Variations

Surely one of the best roasts? It's certainly my favourite, and I love to have a few variations up my sleeve for cooking a roast chicken. These four variations roughly translate to Italian, Spanish, North African and Chinese, but all are accessible when it comes to ingredients and level of skill needed. There are many ways to roast a whole bird, but I find this straightforward method works every time, giving crisp golden skin with moist and juicy meat. As with most ingredients, the better the quality, the better the flavour, so buy the best quality your budget allows.

SERVES 4

1 medium chicken (about
    1.6kg)
50ml olive oil or 50g soft
    unsalted butter, flavoured
    as you wish, see page 92
Salt and freshly ground
    black pepper
Flavourings to fill chicken
    cavity, see page 92
Water or chicken stock

Preheat the oven to 220°C (200°C fan).

Rub the chicken with the olive oil or flavoured butter, pushing some of the oil or butter between the flesh and skin (taking care not to tear the skin). Season generously, inside and out, with salt and pepper, then place in a roasting tin and add any flavourings to the cavity.

Pour 1cm depth of water or stock into the bottom of the tin and put into the oven for 1 hour to 1 hour 20 minutes, or until the juices run clear when you push a skewer into a juicy part of the chicken leg. Alternatively, if one of the chicken legs can be easily pulled off, it's done; if there's a bit of resistance it probably needs a bit longer.

About 10 minutes before the end of cooking, turn up the oven to its highest setting to help crisp the skin. Add a splash of water to the pan if it has dried out and keep an eye that it doesn't catch and burn.

Leave the chicken to rest for 20 minutes before carving; strain any cooking juices to serve with the carved chicken or to make gravy.

Continues overleaf.

Flavours to add to olive oil or butter:

1. Finely grated zest and juice of ½ lemon, 1 crushed garlic clove, chopped thyme, tarragon or rosemary

2. ½ teaspoon each of smoked paprika, ground cumin, ground fennel seeds, dried oregano and 2 crushed garlic cloves

3. ½ teaspoon each of ground cinnamon, ground cardamom, ground coriander, ground black pepper, ground nutmeg

4. 1 teaspoon Chinese five spice, 1 crushed garlic clove, 2 teaspoon grated fresh ginger, 1 teaspoon soy sauce

Flavours to add to cavity:

1. ½ lemon, cut into wedges, 1 whole garlic clove and small bunches of thyme, tarragon or rosemary

2. 2 whole garlic cloves and 2 bay leaves

3. ½ cinnamon stick, 2 bay leaves, ½ lemon, cut into wedges, ½ small onion, sliced

4. 1 whole star anise, ½ cinnamon stick, 1 whole garlic clove, 2 slices of fresh ginger

Serve the chicken with:

1. Aioli, sautéed or roasted potatoes and green salad

2. Chickpeas heated with diced chorizo, roasted cabbage wedges and Romesco Sauce (see page 142)

3. Herbed couscous with dried fruit, yogurt sauce and harissa

4. Steamed greens, steamed rice or noodles and chilli sauce

Ham with Plum Jam and Mustard Glaze

Ham with a shiny golden glaze is a winning combination of sticky, sweet and salty deliciousness. A Christmas must, ham served just so is a superb dish to serve throughout the year, using any seasonal fruits to cut through the savouriness of the cooked ham. Try plum jam with fresh plums or apricot jam with fresh apricots, Spanish membrillo paste and fresh quince, or rhubarb jam and fresh rhubarb. Marmalade works beautifully too, perhaps with some thick slices of orange. Serve the sliced ham with a simple slaw of thinly sliced cabbage, carrots and onion dressed with a little crème fraîche and some Dijon mustard, with boiled potatoes on the side. Leftovers are never a problem!

SERVES ABOUT 12

3–4kg ham on the bone
(ask the butcher to remove
the rind if possible)
100g plum jam, plus an extra
2 tbsp for the plums
120ml apple juice or water
40g brown sugar
1 tbsp Dijon mustard
¼ tsp cayenne pepper or
chilli powder
Approx. 1 tbsp whole cloves
20g butter
12 plums, cut in half and
stones removed

Before roasting the ham, either soak it in cold water overnight, or poach it in a deep pot covered with water for half an hour or so, then drain and pat dry.

Preheat the oven to 170°C (160°C fan).

If it hasn't been done already, remove the rind from the ham in one piece, leaving as much fat behind as you can, and use a sharp knife to score the fat in a diamond pattern. Place the ham in a large baking dish and bake for about 1 hour to colour the fat.

Mix the jam, apple juice or water, brown sugar, mustard and cayenne pepper or chilli powder in a small saucepan. Simmer for 5 minutes until the glaze has thickened slightly.

Brush the ham with half the glaze and stud with the cloves in the middle of each diamond shape in the fat. Bake for about 1 hour more, basting with the reserved glaze every 20 minutes.

Meanwhile, heat the extra 2 tablespoons of jam and the butter in a saucepan, until simmering. Add the plums and simmer on a low heat for 8–10 minutes until tender, then put to one side to cool to room temperature.

Leave the ham to rest for 20 minutes, then slice (removing whole cloves as you go) and serve with the cooked plums.

Venison with Chestnuts, Pumpkin and Pancetta

When the days shorten, this is the perfect autumn roast and will make a welcome change
to your usual Sunday offering. In fact, you may well find yourself cooking venison
on many Sundays throughout autumn and winter when it's in season and at its best.
Wrapping the venison in bacon or pancetta helps to baste this lean meat with flavourful
fat as the joint roasts. You want the meat pink to serve, so a fast roast, followed by a
lengthy rest in a warm spot in your kitchen. Leftover venison is delicious cold, thinly
sliced and served with soft lettuce leaves and pickles – perhaps in a sandwich the next day.

SERVES 4

700g boneless venison
haunch or loin
Salt and freshly ground
black pepper
6 slices of pancetta or
streaky bacon
4 tbsp vegetable oil
4 celery stalks, finely
chopped (and a few finely
chopped celery leaves if
available)
1 onion, finely chopped
400g pumpkin or butternut
squash, peeled and
chopped
20g butter
200g cooked chestnuts,
roughly chopped
2 tsp finely chopped thyme,
rosemary or sage leaves
100ml Marsala or Madeira or
red wine
50ml double cream (or use
cold diced butter)

Preheat the oven to 220°C (200°C fan).

Season the venison with salt and pepper and wrap in the pancetta, tying it into place (or get a butcher to do this for you).

Heat 2 tablespoons of the oil in a frying pan or flameproof roasting tin over a high heat and brown the venison quickly until coloured all over.

Place half the celery and half the onion tightly around the meat and roast in the oven for 15 minutes.

Season the pumpkin with salt and pepper, place in a separate roasting tin and toss in the remaining 2 tablespoons of oil; roast in the oven for about 15 minutes or until tender, then keep warm.

Meanwhile, heat the butter in a frying pan and fry the rest of the onion and celery for about 15 minutes, until golden brown and soft, adding the chestnuts for the last 5 minutes. Add the chopped herbs and celery leaves and season to taste with salt and pepper.

Turn the oven down to 180°C (170°C fan) and continue roasting the venison for another 15 minutes.

Remove from the oven, transfer the meat to a plate and cover it with foil to rest for at least 15 minutes.

Add the Madeira to the venison roasting tin and boil until reduced by half. Add the cream (or whisk in the diced butter) and bring to the boil, then strain into a jug, pressing to extract as much sauce as possible.

Serve the chestnut mix spooned over the pumpkin; slice the venison thinly and serve topped with the pancetta, with the sauce drizzled over the top.

Mushroom, Cheese and Whole Grain Bake

This could be served as a spellbinding vegetarian roast, or used as an accompaniment for other Sunday dishes. I like to use at least two different whole grains, as this gives a more interesting texture and deeper flavour; you can use as many as you like, or just the one if you prefer. Use any mushroom you like; cheese too, for that matter. For a vegan option, leave out the cheese (you could try adding smoked tofu in its place) and use olive oil instead of the butter.

SERVES 4

300g mixed whole grains
   (pearl barley, spelt,
   quinoa, buckwheat)
Salt and freshly ground
   black pepper
50g butter or 50ml olive oil,
   plus extra to grease
2 onions, finely chopped
2 leeks, finely sliced
2 garlic cloves, finely
   chopped
450g mushrooms (mixed
   or wild, oyster, chestnut,
   flat, button), cut into
   similar-sized pieces
1 tbsp soy sauce
2 tbsp sage or rosemary
   leaves, finely chopped
125g cheese (Parmesan,
   Cheddar), grated
100g soft breadcrumbs
Grated zest of 1 lemon
Small bunch of parsley,
   finely chopped

Preheat the oven to 180°C (170°C fan) and butter a baking dish (approx. 25 x 30cm).

Cook the grains with a pinch of salt in boiling water until tender, about 30–40 minutes, then drain and keep to one side.

Meanwhile, heat half the butter in a large saucepan and cook the onions, leeks and garlic until soft, about 10 minutes. Then mix through the cooked grains.

Fry the mushrooms in the remaining butter for 5 minutes, or until they have released their liquid and it has evaporated, then add to the grain mix with the soy sauce; add salt and pepper to taste.

Mix through the sage or rosemary, grated cheese and half the breadcrumbs.

Spread over the baking dish then gently press down with the back of a spoon. Mix the remaining breadcrumbs with the lemon zest and parsley and sprinkle over the mushroom mix.

Cover with foil and bake for 30 minutes, then uncover and bake for 15 minutes until it's hot throughout and browning on top. Serve immediately, in big spoonfuls.

Stuffed Pumpkin

These individual roast pumpkins are a great way to use any attractive small pumpkins and squashes you see on sale in the autumn. This recipe will work well enough with a larger pumpkin but you will need to increase the roasting times a little, until the pumpkin flesh can be easily pierced with a skewer. These can be prepared beforehand and popped in the oven to heat through later, making them an ideal, panic-free and impressive supper option.

SERVES 4

150g brown rice, rinsed and
    drained (or use white rice
    if you prefer)
Salt and freshly ground
    black pepper
4 small winter squash or
    pumpkins, each about the
    size of a large grapefruit
5 tbsp extra virgin olive oil
4 fresh bay leaves
4 garlic cloves, peeled and
    left whole
2 red onions, finely chopped
3 celery stalks, finely
    chopped
150g cooked chestnuts,
    roughly chopped
1 tbsp chopped fresh thyme
120g soft blue cheese
    (dolcelatte, gorgonzola,
    Roquefort), chopped into
    cubes (or use other soft
    cheese, such as goat)

Preheat the oven to 190°C (180°C fan).

Boil the brown rice in twice its volume of lightly salted water for about 45 minutes or until just tender. Leave to rest for 10 minutes, then drain well and put to one side.

Meanwhile, cut the squash tops off about 3cm down. Use a spoon to scoop out the seeds and discard, reserving the tops.

Rub the squash all over with about 1 tablespoon of the olive oil and season the insides generously with salt and pepper, then add a bay leaf and a garlic clove to each along with a teaspoon of olive oil. Place in a roasting tin with the lids alongside and roast for about 45 minutes until soft.

Heat the remaining 3 tablespoons of olive oil in a pan and fry the onions and celery for 10 minutes until soft.

Add the chestnuts and thyme to the onions and continue to cook for about 5 minutes, until the mix is quite sticky, then stir through the cooked rice. Add the cheese and season to taste with salt and pepper.

Remove the bay leaves from the roasted squash (keep the garlic inside) and divide the onion and rice mixture among the squash (they can be prepared to this point and set aside to cook later).

Return to the oven and bake for 15 minutes or until the filling is hot and the cheese has melted. Serve immediately.

BARBECUES

Forget about inclement weather forecasts, the great British barbecue is a halcyon time where it's all blue skies and lovely lawns. It's a primal activity when we light fires and cook food over smoking embers, but there's so much more to a good barbecue than a couple of beers and hunks of steak. Cooking on the barbecue can really make ingredients shine, firing up their flavours and emboldening them with a good, smoky attitude.

Butterflied Lamb Leg with Preserved Lemon Dressing

A boned, butterflied leg of lamb is just about the easiest way to barbecue a big joint of meat. When butterflied, the meat will also take to marinating very well indeed. Harissa is a boon in any kitchen – this north-African chilli paste is a thunderbolt of flavour. Serve with steamed couscous or warm flatbreads, together with a great big green salad.

SERVES 8

2 tbsp harissa
2 tbsp extra virgin olive oil
3 garlic cloves, crushed
Juice of ½ lemon
1 leg of lamb (about 1.5kg),
    boned and butterflied
    (see Tip below)
Salt

Preserved lemon dressing

2 preserved lemons, flesh
    and pith discarded, skin
    finely chopped
4 tbsp extra virgin olive oil
Juice of ½ lemon
Small bunch of coriander,
    roughly chopped

In a large bowl, mix together the harissa, olive oil, garlic and lemon juice. Add the lamb and coat in the marinade, cover and leave in the fridge overnight (or at least 2 hours, or up to 24 hours).

To make the dressing, roughly blend the preserved lemon, olive oil and the lemon juice, then stir through the coriander.

Before cooking, bring the meat back to room temperature and season with salt.

Prepare your grill or coals for both high and indirect heat so you can move the lamb depending on how much heat you need at different points. Barbecue for about 10 minutes on each side, or until nicely pink (cook longer for more well done meat), avoiding flare-ups and scorching as much as possible, and moving to indirect heat if needed.

Once the lamb is cooked, spoon the preserved lemon dressing over and cover loosely with foil; leave to rest for 10 minutes, then slice and serve.

Butterflying a leg of lamb

Ask your butcher to butterfly the leg if you're not up to the challenge or follow this explanation:

With the lamb leg on a board, you should see three distinct lines denoting the three muscles making up the whole leg. Using a sharp knife, cut along these lines to open out the lamb leg – you want the outside of the leg to lie flat on the board. Cut away any sinew. Slash any thicker sections of meat to give an even thickness across the whole piece of meat. Lay a piece of clingfilm or baking parchment over the meat and firmly hit with a rolling pin to flatten it slightly.

Steak Sandwich

. . . .

This is a beast of a sandwich, ideal for a big appetite. You could cook this indoors in a pan or in a very hot oven, but there is something hugely satisfying about seeing (and smelling) steak on the barbecue. Best eaten outside and probably not in your best dress or shirt, you'll need a mountain of paper napkins. I would recommend a cold beer in your other hand.

2 garlic cloves, crushed

½ tsp chilli flakes

1 tsp dried oregano

1 tsp paprika

1 tsp coarsely ground
    black pepper

2 tbsp olive oil

2 tbsp red wine vinegar

600g rump steaks, cut about
    2cm thick

1 red onion, thinly sliced

2 red peppers, thinly sliced

Salt and freshly ground black
    pepper

4 large crusty rolls – the
    bigger the better

60g butter, softened

8 slices of cheese (one that
    melts well)

Your favourite chilli sauce,
    to serve (optional)

In a bowl, mix together the garlic, spices and 1 tablespoon each of the olive oil and vinegar. Add the meat and leave for a few hours (but not longer than 8 hours).

Heat the remaining olive oil in a frying pan over a high heat and fry the onion and peppers for about 5 minutes, then add the remaining vinegar and cook over a high heat until it has fully evaporated. Season to taste with salt and pepper.

Preheat the grill or barbecue to hot.

Split the rolls lengthways, keeping them joined at one side. Butter them and place each roll, cut-side up, on a piece of foil, folding the sides down and twisting the ends to make a 'foil boat' around the bread. Place a slice of cheese in each roll and top with peppers and onions and another slice of cheese. Place on the edge of the barbecue to warm through.

Season the meat with salt and grill until well browned on the outside but still juicy inside, then remove and cut into thin slices. Put on top of the cheese in the rolls.

Return the sandwiches in their foil boats to the barbecue (closing the lid if there is one). Cook for about 2–3 minutes, then serve, with chilli sauce if you like.

Brick Chicken with Garlic

This method for grilling might sound (and certainly look) a bit unusual, but it benefits the chicken in various ways: the pressure of something heavy on the meat will press more of the skin on to the grill, resulting in a crisper skin, and the pressure will give a firmer texture to the cooked meat. The brick will also conduct heat into the top of the bird, meaning that it cooks more uniformly. You can cook any bone-in chicken pieces with this method (thighs, leg), but reduce the weight – perhaps a heavy pan lid instead of a brick. Serve with a green salad and crusty bread or some boiled new potatoes.

1 whole chicken
(about 1.5kg), backbone
removed or spatchcocked
(ask your butcher to do
this if you prefer)
4 tbsp olive oil
Salt and freshly ground
black pepper
1 sprig of rosemary, leaves
removed and finely
chopped
2 garlic cloves, crushed
Finely grated zest and juice
of ½ lemon

Wrap two bricks in foil. Prepare your grill or coals for both high and indirect heat so you can move the chicken depending on how much heat you need at different points.

Place the chicken on a work surface, skin-side up. Using your palms, press firmly on the breastbone to flatten the breast. Rub the chicken with 2 tablespoons of the oil and season with salt and pepper.

Tuck the wings slightly under the breast. Place the chicken, skin-side down, over the hotter side of the grill. Place the bricks on top of the chicken and cook until the skin browns and crisps, 10–15 minutes, keeping an eye on it and moving it to a cooler part of the grill if it begins to burn.

Meanwhile, mix the rosemary, garlic, lemon zest and juice and the remaining 2 tablespoons of olive oil.

Use tongs to remove the bricks. Turn the chicken skin-side up and brush with about half of the rosemary and garlic mix.

Move the chicken to a cooler part of the grill, replace the bricks and continue grilling until the chicken is cooked through, about 20–25 minutes. To test, push a skewer into the thickest part of a leg: the juices should run clear.

Place the chicken in a dish, spoon over the rest of the rosemary and garlic mix and wrap the dish in foil. Leave to rest in a warm place for 10–20 minutes before chopping into pieces (on the bone) and serving.

Jerk Skewers

The smell of traditional jerk cooking in a huge drum barbecue – in the Caribbean or closer to home at a carnival – really gets the mouth watering. You can recreate the flavours quite well with this domestic version. You could use any fresh hot chilli, but Scotch bonnet are worth seeking out. Take care when handling the chilli, and keep the seeds in the chilli if you want more heat. Serve with rice, chopped avocado, Tabasco or any hot chilli sauce and plenty of lime wedges.

1 tsp salt
1½ tsp ground allspice
1 tsp ground ginger or
    1 tbsp grated fresh ginger
1 tsp freshly ground
    black pepper
½ tsp ground cinnamon
1 tsp dried thyme, or
    2 tsp chopped fresh
    thyme
½ bunch of spring onions,
    finely chopped
3 garlic cloves, peeled
1 Scotch bonnet chilli,
    deseeded and finely
    chopped
1 tbsp brown sugar
1 tbsp soy sauce
Juice of 1 lime, plus lime
    wedges to serve
600–800g pork or chicken,
    cut into approx.
    4cm cubes

Blend all of the ingredients (apart from the meat) to a coarse paste.

Put the meat in a bowl, mix with the spice paste and leave in the fridge to marinate for at least an hour – up to 24 hours is fine.

If using wooden skewers, soak them in water for 30 minutes.

Thread the marinated meat on to the skewers.

Preheat the grill or barbecue to hot.

Cook the skewers for about 5 minutes on each side, until the meat is charred on the outside and fully cooked through. Serve immediately.

Stuffed Portobello Mushroom Burgers

Veggie burgers get terrible press, and it's a shame. Make these and everyone will be impressed, vegetarians and carnivores alike. You can serve them as a side dish, but why not serve these delicious burgers loud and proud? Mushrooms are a winner for any barbecue because they're succulent and juicy – almost impossible to dry out as they cook. You can prepare these well in advance. If you have vegan guests, omit the butter and cheese, and bump the flavour with chopped fresh herbs, smoked tofu in lieu of the cheese, chilli flakes, and a final drizzle of good olive oil.

12 Portobello mushrooms, stems removed and reserved

Vegetable or olive oil, for brushing

Salt and freshly ground black pepper

40g butter or 3 tbsp olive oil

4 shallots or 2 small red onions, finely chopped

2 garlic cloves, finely chopped

Small bunch of flat-leaf parsley, finely chopped

200g halloumi (or other salty hard cheese), coarsely grated (or use smoked tofu)

Squeeze of lemon juice

4 burger buns or ciabatta rolls, to serve

Big handful of rocket or watercress, to serve

4 tbsp aioli, mustard or garlic mayonnaise, to serve

Preheat the oven to 180°C (170°C fan).

Brush eight of the mushrooms all over with oil, then season with salt and pepper and roast for 10 minutes, until just cooked, but still holding their shape.

Finely chop the other four mushrooms and all the stems.

Heat the butter or oil in a frying pan and fry the shallots and garlic for 5 minutes until soft. Add the chopped mushrooms and a big pinch of salt and cook for about 5 minutes, until the mushrooms have released their liquid.

Raise the heat a bit and cook until the liquid has evaporated, about 2 minutes. Stir in the parsley, cheese and a squeeze of lemon juice and season with salt and pepper to taste. Fill four of the cooked whole mushrooms with the mix and place another on top to enclose the filling. These can be kept in the fridge until ready to grill.

Preheat the grill or barbecue to hot.

When ready to cook, brush the stuffed mushrooms with a little more oil and grill for about 5 minutes on each side until heated through, taking care when turning over not to spill any of the filling.

Serve in buns with rocket and garlic mayonnaise.

Mussels on the Barbecue with Herby Breadcrumbs

Using the smoky heat of the barbecue is a glorious way to cook these sweet, juicy shellfish – with the garlicky, herby breadcrumbs, what's not to love? Cook these mussels as an additional dish to other barbecue items. Surf and turf? Take a well-earned bow!

1–2 lemons
40ml extra virgin olive oil
50g fresh breadcrumbs
4 garlic cloves, finely
  chopped
Small bunch of flat-leaf
  parsley, finely chopped
2 sprigs of thyme or
  rosemary, coarsely
  chopped
Salt and freshly ground
  black pepper
About 40 mussels, scrubbed
  and beards removed
  (see Tip on page 68 and
  discard any that are open
  or broken)

Preheat the grill or barbecue to medium.

Grate the zest of ½ a lemon and put to one side; cut the lemons in half.

Heat half the olive oil in a pan and fry the breadcrumbs for about 5 minutes, until golden brown all over. Tip on to a plate and put to one side.

Add the remaining oil and the garlic to the pan and stir the garlic with a wooden spoon so it flavours the oil; do not let the garlic brown. Stir in the fried breadcrumbs, herbs and grated lemon zest, season with salt and pepper to taste and put to one side.

When the barbecue is hot, have a pair of tongs and a big deep serving dish to hand.

Start grilling the lemons, cut-side down, until they are caramelised. At the same time, scatter the mussels on the barbecue in a single layer. As the mussels open, use the tongs to remove them from the grill to the serving dish. Discard any mussels that do not open.

Squeeze the juice from the caramelised lemons over the mussels and spoon the breadcrumb mixture into the shells. Serve immediately.

Quick Pork Ribs

Barbecued pork ribs are an art form in America's Deep South. While some recipes have the ribs cooked until the meat falls off the bone, I like to retain a bit of chewy bite. This is sticky-fingers, greedy-chops eating – maybe not one for a first date!

2.5kg pork ribs in one piece
Salt
4 tbsp vegetable oil
2 onions, finely chopped
4 garlic cloves, roughly
    chopped
1 fresh green chilli, finely
    chopped
2 tsp cayenne pepper or
    chilli powder (less if you
    want it less hot)
1 tbsp smoked paprika
1 tsp ground fennel
1 tsp ground mace or nutmeg
1 tsp ground coriander
4 tbsp soft brown sugar
4 tbsp maple syrup or honey
4 tbsp cider vinegar
300ml water
Small bunch of coriander,
    roughly chopped
    (optional)

To cook the ribs, place them in a pot with cold, heavily salted water (seawater level) to cover. Bring to the boil, skim the scum from the surface, then reduce the heat, cover the pan and simmer until just tender, about 45 minutes.

While the ribs are cooking, heat the oil in a large saucepan and fry the onions, garlic and green chilli until golden brown, about 15 minutes.

Add the spices, sugar, maple syrup or honey, cider vinegar and water. Bring to the boil, then reduce the heat and simmer for 30 minutes. Leave to cool slightly, then blend until smooth.

Preheat the grill or barbecue to hot and have long tongs to hand.

Drain the ribs and lay them on the grill; baste with the sauce, then flip and baste the other side. Keep glazing and flipping the ribs until sticky and charred – you have to work quite quickly.

Place the ribs on a chopping board and give them a final brush of the sauce. Sprinkle with the coriander (if using). Chop into individual ribs and serve with a huge pile of paper napkins.

Tandoori Lamb with Mint Raita and Mango Salsa

Traditional tandoori served with a fresh, zingy mango salsa – a great alternative to sticky mango chutney. This is the sort of meal to eat outdoors with the sunshine on your back in the company of your very favourite friends and family.

200g plain yogurt

3 tbsp tandoori spice blend

Salt and freshly ground black pepper

500g lamb, cut into approx. 4cm cubes (or use chicken)

2 garlic cloves, crushed to a paste

2 tsp grated fresh ginger

1 lemon, halved

1 red onion: ½ cut into wedges, ½ finely chopped

1 red pepper: ½ cut into squares, ½ finely chopped

12 mint leaves, finely chopped

1 mango (ripe, but not overripe), peeled, stoned and finely chopped

Naan breads or rice, to serve

In a bowl, mix 50g of the yogurt with the tandoori spice and salt and pepper to taste, then mix in the lamb, garlic, ginger and a squeeze of lemon juice. Put in the fridge for at least 2 hours or overnight.

If using wooden skewers, soak them in water for at least 30 minutes.

Thread the lamb, onion wedges and pepper squares on to the skewers.

Mix the mint leaves and a squeeze of lemon juice with the remaining yogurt and put to one side.

Mix the mango, finely chopped onion and pepper with the juice of ½ the lemon, season with salt to taste and put to one side.

Preheat the grill or barbecue to hot.

Grill the kebabs, turning frequently, for about 8 minutes, or until the lamb is cooked. Serve with the mango salsa, the mint raita and naan breads or rice.

Merguez-Spiced Patties

These burger patties have all the delicious flavours of spicy North African merguez sausages. You could cook them in a frying pan, but a bit of smoky flavour from the barbecue really gives them the edge. While you've got the barbecue fired up, it's worth slinging some extra veg on the hot grill to accompany these spicy patties: try courgettes and peppers cut into broad batons and/or aubergine cut into 2cm slices, drizzled with a little olive oil and given a good pinch of salt.

600g minced lamb or beef
Salt and freshly ground
    black pepper
120g Greek yogurt
6 dates, pitted and chopped
12 mint leaves, finely
    chopped
½ lemon
½ cucumber, peeled,
    deseeded and finely
    chopped
½ red onion, finely chopped
2 ripe tomatoes, finely
    chopped
4 burger buns or
    4 flatbreads, split open

Quick harissa
1 tsp ground cumin
1 tsp ground coriander
½–1 tsp chilli powder
1 tbsp paprika
1 tbsp lemon juice
2 garlic cloves, roughly
    chopped
1–2 fresh red chillies
    (seeds removed if you
    don't want it too hot)

To make the harissa, blend the spices, lemon juice, the garlic and chillies to a coarse paste.

Stir 2 tablespoons of the harissa paste into the minced meat, along with 1 teaspoon of salt and ½ teaspoon of pepper, and mix until evenly distributed. Shape the meat into four patties (slightly larger in diameter than the burger buns, if using).

Mix the remaining harissa paste with the yogurt, dates, mint and a squeeze of lemon juice and salt and pepper to taste.

Mix the cucumber, onion and tomatoes with a squeeze of lemon juice and salt and pepper to taste.

Preheat the grill or barbecue to hot.

Grill the patties until cooked to your liking (about 5–8 minutes for medium), turning once.

Warm the flatbreads or burger buns lightly on the grill. Spread the yogurt mix inside, insert the burgers and spoon in the cucumber salad.

Pork Chops with Spiced Tomato Marinade

This deeply flavoured marinade, with two types of paprika, cumin and allspice, gives a satisfying smoky crust to these chops. The addition of orange and lime juice cuts beautifully through these intensely savoury flavours. Use the same marinade for other meats if you like – chicken, lamb or beef will all work well. Serve with the Mexican-Style Grilled Corn (see page 114) or a green salad dressed with lime and plenty of chopped fresh coriander.

150g ripe cherry tomatoes

2 garlic cloves, peeled and left whole

1 fresh red chilli, split in half lengthways and stem removed

1 tsp sweet unsmoked paprika

1 tsp sweet or hot smoked paprika

¼ tsp freshly ground cumin

¼ tsp freshly ground allspice

1 tsp brown sugar or honey

Salt and freshly ground black pepper

1 tbsp olive oil or vegetable oil

Juice of 1 orange

Juice of 1 lime, plus 1 lime, cut into wedges, to serve

4 thick pork chops

1 small red onion, thinly sliced, to serve

100g radishes, finely sliced, to serve

Small bunch of coriander, roughly chopped

Heat the grill to high and grill the tomatoes, garlic and fresh chilli on a foil-lined tray for about 5–10 minutes, until starting to char.

Remove and place in a blender or food processor with the spices, sugar or honey, and salt and pepper to taste; blend to a coarse paste. Heat the oil in a pan and fry the paste for about 5 minutes until thickened. Stir in the orange and lime juices and leave to cool.

Put the pork chops in a bowl, add half the paste and marinate in the fridge overnight (or for at least 2 hours).

Preheat the grill or barbecue to hot.

Grill the chops for 4–6 minutes on each side or until just cooked through, basting twice with the reserved marinade paste. Cover with foil and leave to rest for at least 5 minutes.

Serve topped with onion, radishes and coriander, with lime wedges on the side.

Mexican-Style Grilled Corn

This recipe is a nod to the popular Mexican street food, where vendors slather the grilled corn in garlic, mayonnaise and strong cheese. It is a salty, sweet, spicy, rich and tangy assault on the taste buds. Eaten whole, you'll need plenty of napkins and nimble fingers. Alternatively, once cooked, shuck the corn off the ears and hurl these outrageously tasty nuggets into salads, or even on toast!

2 tsp chilli flakes

1 garlic clove, crushed

4 tbsp mayonnaise

8 ears of corn, husked

Vegetable oil, for brushing

Salt and freshly ground
　　black pepper

8 tbsp (about 100g) coarsely
　　grated or crumbled
　　strong salty cheese (feta,
　　Parmesan, Cheddar)

Small bunch of coriander,
　　finely chopped

1 lime, cut into wedges

Preheat the grill or barbecue to medium.

Mix the chilli and garlic into the mayonnaise. Put to one side.

Brush the corn with oil and season with salt and pepper. Grill, using tongs to turn occasionally, until cooked through and lightly charred, about 10 minutes.

Remove from the grill and either skewer or insert corn forks, then immediately brush each ear with ½ tablespoon of the mayonnaise. Sprinkle with cheese, coriander, and extra chilli if you like. Squeeze lime over each ear and serve.

Tamarind and Chilli Prawns: Two Flavours

Tamarind is used in Thai, Mexican and southern Indian cooking, lending a pleasing sweet-sour flavour to dishes, and the idea here is that a marinade made with tamarind can easily be adapted for two different recipes. Do try to buy block tamarind rather than the ready-made paste, which tends to be a bit salty and overly processed-tasting. Simply break off a piece of the block (roughly equal to the weight of pulp in the recipe), place in a small bowl and cover with hot water to soften. Soak for about 15 minutes, then mix well and push the paste through a sieve to remove any stones or fibrous matter. This marinade will also work with chicken wings.

300g large raw peeled prawns
1 bunch of spring onions,
    cut into 4cm lengths
    (optional)

Tamarind marinade base
60g sieved tamarind pulp,
    or use 4 tbsp lime juice
2 garlic cloves, crushed
3 tbsp vegetable oil
Salt and freshly ground
    black pepper

Smoky flavouring
½–1 tsp chipotle chilli
    powder, or hot smoked
    paprika to taste
1 tsp sugar

Thai flavouring
1 tbsp soft light brown sugar
1 tbsp Thai fish sauce
2 tbsp grated fresh ginger
1 tsp hot chilli flakes or
    1 finely chopped fresh
    red chilli

Combine the base marinade ingredients in a large bowl with about ½ teaspoon each of salt and pepper. Stir through either the smoky or Thai flavourings, then add the prawns and marinate in the fridge for at least 30 minutes and up to 8 hours (or overnight).

If using bamboo or wooden skewers, soak them in water for at least 30 minutes.

Preheat the grill or barbecue to medium.

Thread the prawns and spring onions (if using) on to skewers and grill for about 1–2 minutes on each side, or until just cooked and charred.

Serve with rice or in wraps.

PICNICS

A good picnic is a clever picnic. Serve a joyous and diverse spread to your guests, abandoning the usual sandwiches and instead choosing some of these recipes to create a really memorable feast. With a little forward planning and preparation, these dishes can be assembled on the picnic blanket with a final al fresco flourish, or indeed can make for a quick lunch at home if the weather isn't playing ball.

Three Pickled Eggs

These eggs make terrific party snacks and add colour to picnics. Pickle your eggs three ways and you will be met with wonderfully varied outcomes. Try cracking the boiled eggs all over but not peeling the shells before immersing them in the pickle juice. When it comes to serving your eggs, peel off the shells and they will be beautifully marbled.

6 eggs, hard-boiled and peeled

Basic pickle
200ml water
200ml white wine vinegar
50g sugar
1 garlic clove, sliced
3 bay leaves, fresh or dried
½ tsp salt

Pink
1 raw beetroot, peeled and sliced
1 tsp fennel seeds
1 tsp mustard seeds
4 allspice berries
8 black peppercorns

Tea
2 tbsp soy sauce
2 slices of fresh ginger
1 tea bag
½ tsp Sichuan or black peppercorns
1 dried red chilli

Herb and chilli
1 small red onion, sliced
1 tsp coriander seeds
1 tsp nigella seeds
2 tsp dried dill
½ cinnamon stick
1 dried red chilli
½ tsp unsmoked paprika

Wash a large jar (big enough to hold 6 eggs) and its lid in hot soapy water, rinse and dry well. If you want to keep the eggs for more than 5 or 6 days, it's a good idea to sterilise the jar: place in a preheated oven at 110°C for about 10–15 minutes. Alternatively, put the jar through a hot cycle in the dishwasher.

Put all of the basic pickle ingredients into a saucepan and bring to the boil. Add the extra flavourings and leave to infuse and cool.

Put the eggs in the jar. Pour the spiced vinegar and all the flavourings over the eggs and seal. Give the jar a gentle shake to ensure the eggs are fully surrounded by the pickle.

Keep in the fridge for at least 4 days before serving; these will keep for up to 3 weeks.

Spanish Tortilla

Tortilla is the ultimate in portable food. Straight up, with soft cooked onions and potatoes and eggs, a good tortilla is always a triumph. You can, of course, embellish the trio by adding other egg-friendly ingredients – shredded ham (Serrano would be ideal here, sticking with the Spanish theme), chunks of chorizo or sliced, roasted peppers. A generous hand with the olive oil is needed for this recipe. However, the oil can be drained and re-used to cook more tortillas, or even for dressings. Practice makes perfect.

1 onion, finely sliced
250ml extra virgin olive oil
650g waxy potatoes, peeled
    and very thinly sliced
6 eggs, beaten
Salt and freshly ground
    black pepper

Gently fry the onion in the olive oil in a large frying pan for about 20 minutes (I prepare the potatoes at this point) until soft and just starting to colour.

Rinse and dry the potato slices. When the onion is soft, add the potatoes to the pan and cook until the potato is completely soft, then drain well (reserving the olive oil).

Beat the eggs in a large jug, add the potato and onion mix, season well with salt and pepper, and put to one side for 5 minutes.

Put a frying pan (approx. 22cm diameter) over a medium heat and add a generous tablespoon of the drained olive oil, swirling to coat the base of the pan.

When it is medium hot, add the egg mixture and give the pan a gentle shake to settle the mixture into the pan. Cook for about 4–6 minutes until there is a nice golden brown crust underneath and the tortilla begins to come away from the sides of the pan.

Place a large plate (about 26cm) over the pan, and invert it so the tortilla land on the plate cooked-side up.

Return the pan to the heat and add another tablespoon of oil. Carefully slide the tortilla back into the pan, using a wide spatula to nudge it in and scrape any uncooked egg stuck to the plate. Tuck any untidy edges down and cook for about 3 minutes until it is springy to the touch but still moist (and even a little undercooked) in the middle, taking care not to let it overcook.

Twice-Devilled Eggs

Why devil eggs once when you can devil them twice, first flavouring the yolk, then flavouring the whole egg with another topping? A nifty way to transport the eggs is to place the egg halves in the spaces of an egg box – you'll need 12 paper muffin cases and an extra egg box. Clingfilm the egg boxes and assemble the second toppings with a confident flourish at the picnic.

MAKES 12 DEVILLED EGG HALVES

6 eggs, hard-boiled
    and peeled
4 tbsp mayonnaise,
    preferably homemade
2 tsp softened butter
A few drops of hot sauce
2 tsp Dijon mustard
Salt and freshly ground
    black pepper

Cut the eggs in half lengthways. Scoop out the yolks and mash with a fork.

Beat together the mayonnaise, butter, hot sauce and mustard, then stir in the egg yolk and season with salt and pepper to taste.

Spoon or pipe into the egg whites, arrange on a plate and top with an additional topping before serving.

ADDITIONAL TOPPINGS
Choose one or more of the following
- Sriracha (or other chilli sauce) drizzled to taste, ½ bunch of finely chopped spring onions and toasted sesame seeds
- 1–2 finely chopped fresh green chillies, chopped fresh coriander and a generous pinch of ground cumin, curry powder or garam masala
- 3 rashers of bacon, cooked until crisp then finely chopped, and chopped fresh tarragon or parsley
- 3 slices of smoked salmon, finely chopped, and chopped fresh dill
- 3 finely chopped anchovies, 1 tablespoon freshly grated Parmesan, 1 tablespoon chopped parsley and 2 tablespoons toasted breadcrumbs

Black Pudding Scotch Eggs

Boiled eggs encased in inky, rich pork meat, this is a real crowd pleaser and is straightforward to make. This recipe will make four Scotch eggs, but I would encourage you to double the amounts and make eight. The eggs will keep in the fridge for up to 3 days.

300g good-quality black
  pudding
150g minced pork
200g fresh white
  breadcrumbs
1 tbsp finely chopped parsley
Salt and freshly ground
  black pepper
6 tbsp plain flour, seasoned
  with salt and pepper
1 egg, beaten
4 medium eggs, hard-boiled
  and peeled
Sunflower oil, for
  deep-frying

Mix the black pudding, minced pork, 30g of the breadcrumbs and the parsley until well combined and season well with salt and pepper. Divide the mixture into eight balls, then flatten each ball into a disc about 7cm wide.

Put the flour into a bowl, the beaten egg in another and the remaining breadcrumbs into a third bowl.

Place one disc of meat mixture in the palm of your hand, put a boiled egg in the middle, then top with a second disc. Squeeze, mould and seal the meat mixture around the egg, then repeat with the remaining meat and eggs.

Coat each Scotch egg in flour, then egg and finally in the breadcrumbs. Chill the Scotch eggs until you're ready to cook them.

Pour about 5cm of oil into a large, deep pan and carefully heat to 180°C, or until hot enough to brown a sprinkle of breadcrumbs in about 30 seconds.

Gently lower the Scotch eggs into the oil and fry for 5–8 minutes, turning regularly until golden and crisp. Drain on kitchen paper and leave to rest for about 10 minutes before eating, or leave to cool to room temperature.

New Orleans Muffuletta

Sandwiches are a popular go-to for picnics, but this epic version takes the idea of ingredients in between slices of bread to another level! It is a hollowed-out loaf filled with a delicious mix of charcuterie and cheese that is pressed for a few hours and carried whole to the picnic. Save the scooped-out bread from the middle to make breadcrumbs for another use, such as the Scotch Eggs on page 124.

1 red onion, thinly sliced

2 tbsp olive oil

1 round loaf of bread, about 20cm in diameter

100g roasted red peppers, thinly sliced

Small bunch of parsley, finely chopped

4 tbsp tapenade (or use roughly chopped pitted olives)

2 tbsp red or white wine vinegar

Salt and freshly ground black pepper

150g thinly sliced mortadella or cooked ham

150g thinly sliced chorizo or salami

150g thinly sliced Serrano or Parma ham, or coppa

150g thinly sliced provolone, manchego or pecorino cheese

Fry the onion in the olive oil for 5 minutes until soft.

Meanwhile, slice off the top 5cm of the bread and put to one side. Using a sharp serrated knife, cut around the perimeter of the interior, making sure not to break through the crust, then use your hand to pull out the soft bread from the inside, leaving you with a hollow loaf.

Mix the cooked onion with the red peppers, parsley, tapenade and vinegar, then season with salt and pepper to taste.

Spread half of the pepper mix in the bottom of the hollow loaf. Lay the sliced meats and cheese in alternating layers, top with the remaining pepper mix and replace the top of the bread.

Wrap the sandwich tightly in foil or greaseproof paper, then place in between two chopping boards. Place a heavy weight (about 4kg) on top and leave for at least 2 hours or overnight.

Using a bread knife, slice the sandwich into quarters through the paper or foil, unwrap, and serve.

Ham Baguette with Gherkin and Shallot Butter

Flavoured butters are brilliant for picnics. Prepared in advance, they're the casual ingredient to stuff in a sandwich or roll, delivering flavour like no other. You could certainly add a few lettuce leaves here, but I rather like the simplicity of this sandwich. Baguettes are famous for being at their very best when spanking fresh. Take the baguette with you whole on the picnic and assemble the few ingredients in situ; you'll look spectacularly organised!

50g butter, softened
2 tbsp finely chopped flat-
    leaf parsley or chives
1 shallot, very finely chopped
100g gherkins or cornichons,
    roughly chopped
Salt and freshly ground
    black pepper
1 fresh baguette
4 thick slices of cooked ham

Beat the butter until creamy, then add the herbs, shallot and gherkins, and season to taste with salt and pepper. If you're not using it straight away, keep the butter in the fridge, but let it soften slightly before spreading on bread.

Cut the baguette in half and then in quarters, giving you four long sandwiches. Slice and spread each side with the gherkin and shallot butter. Lay ham slices over the butter and it is ready to serve.

Rainbow Summer Noodles with Tofu and Miso

Tofu has a reputation for being a bit bland – until it's introduced to miso. With bags of savoury (umami) flavour, miso, matched with the clean palette of tofu, is a wonderful combination. This noodle dish is a vibrant jumble of raw vegetables and punchy herbs together with a turbocharged marinade. Perfect picnic food. Fry the tofu and marinate with the spring onion mix in advance, if you like, and assemble the noodles just before setting out for your picnic.

200g dried rice noodles
(or use ready-cooked)
6 tbsp coconut or
vegetable oil
1 bunch of spring onions,
finely sliced
3 garlic cloves
2 tsp brown sugar
2 tbsp finely grated fresh
ginger
Salt
340g extra-firm tofu,
drained, patted dry and cut
into roughly 2cm cubes
2 tbsp white miso paste
(or use light soy sauce)
Juice of 2 limes
2 tbsp white or black sesame
seeds
1 red pepper, deseeded and
thinly sliced
1 cucumber, peeled,
deseeded and thinly sliced
1 carrot, thinly sliced
1 baby gem lettuce, thinly
sliced
Small bunch of coriander or
mint, roughly chopped

If using dried noodles, cook them according to the packet instructions, drain and cool under cold water, then drain again. Toss through 1 teaspoon of oil to stop them sticking.

Roughly chop or blend together the spring onions, garlic, sugar and half the ginger, then fry in 2 tablespoons of the oil for 1 minute or until softened. Season to taste with salt and put into a shallow bowl.

Heat 1 tablespoon of the oil in a frying pan and fry the tofu in a single layer until golden all over, then tip into the bowl with the spring onion mix and toss together to coat.

Mix the miso paste, lime juice, sesame seeds, the rest of the ginger and 2 tablespoons of oil and season to taste. Put to one side.

Toss the tofu through the noodles, then top with the vegetables, followed by the dressing and the herbs.

Smoked Mackerel Roll with Quick Pickled Vegetables and Seaweed Butter

I love the flavour of dried seaweed and, nowadays, it is an ingredient that is readily available in many supermarkets and health shops. Nori sheets, used for wrapping sushi, are terrific crumbled into various salads. If you're lucky enough to find fresh edible seaweed at the seaside, try it with some bacon or mackerel for a beach breakfast with a difference. For this recipe, you'll need dried seaweed to flavour the butter. Make plenty: it will keep well in the fridge and gives a gorgeous salty taste to all kinds of dishes.

60g butter, softened
4 tbsp dried seaweed
Salt and freshly ground
    black pepper
4 long white rolls
4 smoked mackerel fillets,
    skin and bones removed

Pickled vegetables
250g mixed vegetables
    (celery, carrot, fennel),
    thinly sliced
½ tsp salt
100ml white wine vinegar
100ml water
30g sugar
1 garlic clove, halved

First make the pickled vegetables: mix the vegetables with the salt and leave in a colander to drain for 5 minutes.

Put the vinegar, water, sugar and garlic in a pan, bring to the boil, then leave to cool slightly.

Meanwhile, mix the butter and seaweed together and season to taste with salt and pepper.

Squeeze the vegetables in a cloth and toss in the flavoured vinegar. Put to one side to marinate for at least 30 minutes, although it will get better the longer you keep it, up to about 3 days in the fridge.

Spread the rolls with the seaweed butter, then add the mackerel and some of the drained pickled vegetables.

Potted Cheese

If you've ever found yourself wondering what to do with any odds and ends of cheese, then stop right here. Potted cheese can be kept almost indefinitely if well sealed and stored in the fridge. Add some crusty bread and some good tomatoes, and you've got a perfect picnic snack. The flavourings can be adjusted to taste as you blend all the ingredients together, and I would encourage you to experiment. The French version of this is called *fromage fort*, a powerful blend of crushed garlic, wine (red or white) and plenty of ground black pepper.

250g grated cheese
(a mixture of hard cheeses
such as Cheddar, Double
Gloucester, Cheshire and
Lancashire)
100g unsalted butter,
slightly softened
Large pinch of cayenne
pepper
Large pinch of ground mace
1 tsp mustard
2 tbsp sherry, Madeira or
port (optional)
A splash of Worcestershire
sauce (optional)
A splash of Tabasco
(optional)
Melted butter (optional),
to seal

Blend the cheeses and butter to a paste, together with the spices and other flavourings, either using a food processor or mashing and beating with a spoon.

Pot the cheese in ramekins or little jars. Melt enough butter to seal the cheese (although if you plan to eat this within 2 or 3 days it's not really necessary). Spoon a layer of the clear melted butter (leaving the milky residue behind) over the potted cheese.

Leave in the fridge for at least 24 hours before eating, to allow the flavours to combine.

White Bean Dip with Rosemary, Olive Oil and Lemon

For a change from hummus, make this super simple white bean dip, which is just as good as the beige stuff. Stick with the Italian theme and serve this dip as an antipasti along with some black olives, torn mozzarella balls, sliced salami, breadsticks and raw vegetable sticks to swoosh through the mix. You can use any cooked white beans, or use fresh broad beans when in season.

50ml extra virgin olive oil

2 garlic cloves, crushed

2 tsp finely chopped fresh rosemary

Pinch of chilli flakes, plus extra to serve

Grated zest and juice of ½ lemon

400g tin cannellini beans, drained and rinsed

Salt and freshly ground black pepper

In a small pan, gently heat the olive oil with the garlic, rosemary, chilli flakes and lemon zest until it just begins to bubble, then remove from the heat.

Place the beans in a food processor or blender with the lemon juice. Pulse until the beans are roughly chopped – or make the mix smoother if you like.

Transfer the bean mixture to a small bowl. Strain in the rosemary and garlic oil, mix well, and season to taste with salt and pepper. Serve immediately, or store in an airtight container in the fridge for up to 3 days.

Grain, Kale, Toasted Seed and Roasted Vegetable Salad

Cooked whole grains make a nutritious, textured base and are fabulous for soaking up any juices and dressing. Experiment, find a whole grain you especially like, and use in robust salad dishes such as this one. Raw kale be a bit rough in texture; salting it briefly will soften the leaves a little.

200g barley, spelt, quinoa or wheat grains

1 bay leaf

Salt and freshly ground black pepper

600g assorted root vegetables (carrots, kohlrabi, butternut squash, celeriac, parsnips, sweet potato), peeled and chopped into approx. 3cm cubes

1 red onion, roughly chopped

5 tbsp olive oil

2 tbsp chopped fresh thyme

2 bunches of kale (approx. 250g), leaves stripped off and roughly chopped

40g mixed seeds (sesame, sunflower, pumpkin, nigella, poppy)

Grated zest and juice of ½ lemon

Generous handful of rocket, radicchio or flat-leaf parsley, coarsely chopped

Preheat the oven to 220°C (200°C fan) Cook the grains in 1.5 litres of water with the bay leaf and a big pinch of salt, until tender but still chewy. Depending on the variety, they'll take between 30–45 minutes to cook (quinoa takes a bit less time).

While the grains are cooking, toss the root vegetables and onion on a baking tray with 2 tablespoons of olive oil, the thyme, salt and pepper. Roast the vegetables, stirring after 10 minutes, for about 20 minutes, or until cooked through and nicely browned.

Using your fingertips, rub the kale with a pinch of salt for 30 seconds, then put to one side.

Toast the seeds in the oven for 5 minutes.

Drain the grains well, plucking out the bay leaf. Transfer to a bowl and mix in 3 tablespoons of olive oil, the lemon juice and zest and half the toasted seeds.

Squeeze the kale in a cloth to remove excess water and salt.

Stir the roasted vegetables and kale through the grains and check the seasoning, adding salt and pepper to taste. Then top with the chopped leaves or herbs and the rest of the seeds. Serve at room temperature.

ADDITIONAL TOPPINGS
• Toasted and coarsely chopped almonds, hazelnuts or walnuts
• Coarsely chopped dried cranberries, apricots or cherries
• Cubes of feta, or blobs of ricotta

Picnic Meatloaf

Meatloaf is easy and economical to make. If you make it ahead of time and plan on serving it cold, the flavour will improve, which is a bit of boon when it comes to lunch and picnic dishes. Serve with Dijon mustard, mayonnaise and sliced tomato salad; the Pickled Eggs on page 121 would also be nice; crusty bread is a must. Alternatively, serve the meatloaf warm for lunch or supper with some boiled new potatoes, green beans and mustard.

SERVES ABOUT 6

2 tbsp oil or butter
2 onions, finely chopped
1 large carrot, coarsely grated
2 garlic cloves, finely
    chopped
800g minced beef or pork
    (or a mixture of both)
2 eggs, beaten
4 tbsp finely chopped parsley
2 tsp finely chopped fresh
    rosemary or sage leaves
    (or use 1 tsp dried)
1 tbsp mustard
2 tbsp tomato ketchup
¼ a nutmeg, freshly grated
50g fresh breadcrumbs
100ml chicken or vegetable
    stock, or water
30g cheese, grated
Salt and freshly ground
    black pepper

Preheat the oven to 180°C (170°C fan) and line a 900g loaf tin with greaseproof paper.

Heat the oil or butter in a frying pan over medium heat and cook the onions, carrot and garlic for about 10 minutes, or until soft and sweet but not coloured. Remove to a plate and leave to cool.

Place all the ingredients, including the cooled vegetables, in a large mixing bowl and mix very well.

Press the mix into the lined loaf tin and smooth the top, then top with another piece of greaseproof paper. Bake for 1 hour, or until the meatloaf is cooked through. Test by inserting a skewer; the juices should run clear.

Remove the paper and cook for another 15 minutes, until the top is deep golden brown.

Leave to cool in the tin for at least 10 minutes before removing and serving warm; if you are going to serve it cold, leave it to cool completely in the tin (allowing all the juices to be re-absorbed). When it is completely cold, wrap well and store in the fridge for up to three days.

Sausage Rolls

This recipe makes four pretty large sausage rolls, which is how I like them, although you can make smaller sausage rolls and reduce the cooking time accordingly. I think larger sausage rolls retain their juices and keep better if serving later on in the day. Cooked pastry never fares all that well in the fridge, and as such sausage rolls are best eaten on the day they are made. Buy puff pastry made with butter – it really makes a difference.

700g pork mince

100g streaky bacon, finely chopped

100g fresh breadcrumbs

100ml cold chicken stock, or water

1 tbsp finely chopped fresh sage or thyme (or a combination of both)

Pinch of cayenne pepper or chilli powder (optional)

Salt and freshly ground black pepper

400g all-butter puff pastry

1 egg, lightly beaten

Preheat the oven to 180°C (170°C fan) and line a baking tray with greaseproof paper.

Put the pork, bacon, breadcrumbs, stock, herbs and spices in a large bowl with about 1 teaspoon of salt and mix until well combined. Break off a little piece and fry until cooked to check the seasoning, adding more salt, pepper or cayenne to taste.

Roll out the pastry to a rectangle approximately 40 x 25cm and brush with beaten egg.

Shape the meat filling into a long sausage shape and place on the pastry, then fold the pastry over the filling and crimp the edges together using a fork.

Cut into four (or make smaller rolls if you prefer) and brush the tops with beaten egg, then bake for 40–50 minutes until golden brown.

Leave to cool for 10 minutes on the tray before transferring to a wire rack until ready to serve or transport.

EASY DINNER PARTIES

Dinner parties should not be stressful. Inviting your friends around for supper should be a highlight of your weekend. Super food and great wine fuelled by raucous, good-humoured conversation – the trick is in the planning. These recipes can be prepared in advance – come show time, when your guests are ringing the bell, all you'll have to do is add the finishing touches. Choose to serve these dishes on individual plates or great big platters for everyone to dig deep. Effortless entertaining, served with style.

Three Easy Canapés

Three seasonal canapé offerings here. Choose one and serve in bite-sized pieces to feed your guests as they gather to supper. Or make them as full-size toasts and serve as flavoursome starters. All serve 4 as a starter, and up to 8 as canapés.

Ricotta, Grape and Walnut Toast

Roasting grapes intensifies their flavour and alters their texture; soft, juicy, sweet punctuation notes to the creamy ricotta and toasted walnuts. These canapés have a rustic feel, and the combination of taste and texture is knock out. You can roast the grapes and toast the walnuts up to an hour before guests arrive.

200g black grapes

2 tbsp extra virgin olive oil, plus extra to drizzle

2 tsp balsamic vinegar

Salt and freshly ground black pepper

50g walnuts, roughly chopped

1 tbsp honey

2 tsp finely chopped fresh rosemary leaves

4 large slices of sourdough or ciabatta bread

250g ricotta

Small handful of flat-leaf parsley, radicchio or rocket, roughly chopped

Preheat the oven to 180°C (170°C fan). Line a baking tray with baking parchment.

Toss the grapes with 1 tablespoon of the olive oil, the balsamic vinegar and salt and pepper. Roast in the lined tray for about 10 minutes, until sticky and syrupy. Leave to cool.

Toast the walnuts in a hot frying pan until fragrant, then stir in 1 tablespoon of the olive oil, the honey, rosemary and salt and pepper, then tip on to a plate and leave to cool.

Toast the bread, then spread with the ricotta. Top with the grapes and their juices, then scatter with the walnuts and the chopped leaves. Either chop into bite-sized pieces to serve as canapés or leave whole.

Leek and Romesco Sauce Toast

Romesco sauce comes from Catalonia in Spain, where it is traditionally eaten with grilled calçcots, which are a bit like giant spring onions. Romesco also goes brilliantly with cooked leeks. Romesco will keep in the fridge for up to a week and you'll soon find yourself serving it with everything: as a dip with raw vegetables or as a thick sauce with grilled meat or fish.

2 large leeks, white part only, thickly sliced, washed and dried well

1 tbsp extra virgin olive oil

Salt and freshly ground black pepper

4 large slices of sourdough or ciabatta bread

Small handful of flat-leaf parsley, roughly chopped

Romesco sauce

1 large slice of sourdough or ciabatta bread

1 garlic clove, thinly sliced

4 tbsp flaked or whole almonds (or hazelnuts)

150g roasted red peppers (from a jar, or roasted in a hot oven until soft, then deseeded and peeled)

1 tsp red wine vinegar or sherry vinegar

½ tsp paprika (smoked or unsmoked)

Pinch of chilli flakes (optional)

3 tbsp extra virgin olive oil

To make the romesco sauce, toast the bread, remove the crusts, leave to cool, then cut or rip into small pieces. Put the bread in a food processor with the garlic and almonds and process until coarsely ground. Add the roasted peppers, vinegar, paprika and chilli flakes (if using) and process until the mixture is smooth. Add the olive oil in a thin stream until it is fully emulsified. Season with salt and pepper to taste, plus more vinegar if you like, and put to one side.

Toss the leeks in the olive oil and roast, grill or fry, until slightly charred and cooked through. Season with salt and pepper to taste.

Toast the bread. Pile on the leeks, drizzle or spoon the sauce over the leeks and scatter the chopped parsley over the top. Either chop into bite-sized pieces to serve as canapés or leave whole.

Broad Bean, Pea and Mint Toast

This bright and verdant purée is super easy to pull together. Use fresh peas and broad beans when in season; frozen will work just as well, simply skip the cooking step and thaw the vegetables before blitzing. Any leftover purée makes a fabulous sauce to stir through cooked pasta, with some grated Parmesan to serve. You can store it in the fridge for a day or so. Rubbing the toast with garlic is the classic Italian bruschetta method, and it makes for fabulously tasty toast!

150g podded fresh broad beans, peas or a mix of both

3 garlic cloves: 2 peeled and sliced, 1 peeled and left whole

4 tbsp extra virgin olive oil

Grated zest and juice of ½ lemon

15 mint leaves, roughly chopped

Salt and freshly ground black pepper

4 large slices of sourdough or ciabatta bread

100g ricotta (optional)

Boil the broad beans or peas with the sliced garlic in salted water for 4 minutes, then drain and put into a bowl of cold water. When they are cold, drain. If using broad beans, skin any that are larger than a small fingernail.

Roughly blend the peas or broad beans with the olive oil, lemon zest and mint (it doesn't need to be too smooth), then add salt, pepper and lemon juice to taste.

Toast the bread, then rub with the whole garlic and spread with the ricotta (if using). Top with the purée. Either chop into bite-sized pieces to serve as canapés or leave whole.

Mushroom Pierogi

A good dinner-party starter is one that won't have you breaking into a sweat when it's time to serve supper. These little dumplings are the Polish equivalent to Italian ravioli. Give yourself some time and a clear workspace (with the radio on) and these pierogi are easy to assemble. You will need a pastry cutter or a sharp-edged bowl of about 10cm diameter to cut the rolled dough into little rounds. As with most things, practice makes perfect.

SERVES 6

Dough
350g plain or '00' flour, plus extra for dusting
1 egg, lightly beaten
120ml water
2 tbsp sour cream, plus extra to serve

Filling
1 onion, finely chopped
3 tbsp butter, plus extra to fry the pierogi (optional)
2 garlic cloves, finely chopped
250g mushrooms, finely chopped
15g dried mushrooms, rehydrated, drained and finely chopped
Salt and freshly ground black pepper
2 tbsp finely chopped parsley or dill, plus extra to serve
3 tbsp fresh breadcrumbs

Make the dough by mixing all the ingredients together in a large bowl. Knead for a few minutes until the mixture comes together as a soft smooth dough Cover in plastic or a clean tea towel and leave to rest at room temperature for at least 20 minutes.

To make the filling, fry the onion in the butter over medium heat for 5 minutes or until soft.

Add the garlic and cook for 1 minute, then add all the mushrooms. Turn the heat up and cook until the mushrooms give up their water and it has evaporated. Season to taste with salt and pepper and add the herbs and breadcrumbs. Spread on a plate and leave to cool.

On a lightly floured surface, roll out the dough to a thickness of about 3mm. Using a pastry cutter, cut out 10cm rounds of dough (you should get about 30 rounds).

Hold a round of dough in the palm of your hand. Put a teaspoon of the filling in the centre and fold the dough over the filling. Set the dumpling on your well-floured surface and seal it tight by crimping with the tines of a fork or your fingertips. The pierogi can be frozen at this stage (or keep them in the fridge, but they're more likely to stick together), or boiled ready to be reheated in butter later – they may stick so keep them apart using sheets of greaseproof paper.

Boil your pierogi (from frozen is fine) until they float, then continue to boil for 2 minutes (3 minutes from frozen). Alternatively, you can double cook them: boil until they float, then fry in lots of butter.

Serve with sour cream seasoned with salt and pepper and scatter with chopped herbs.

Salt and Pepper Prawns

A big pile of juicy prawns spiked with chilli will surely set your dinner party off with a bang. Sichuan pepper is a terrific addition here: a Chinese ingredient that gives a pleasing tingling, numbing sensation when eaten. Cooking the prawns with the shell on improves their flavour and will help protect the flesh from overcooking. There is also plenty of flavour in the prawn heads if your slurping skills pass muster. Finger bowls with slices of lemon are a must, as is a great big pile of paper napkins.

SERVES 6

2 tsp ground Sichuan pepper (or to taste)

1 tsp cracked black pepper (or to taste)

1 tsp chilli flakes (or to taste)

Salt

4 tbsp cornflour

600g large prawns, shells on (with or without heads)

4 spring onions, finely chopped

3 garlic cloves, finely chopped

Vegetable oil for frying

Combine the Sichuan pepper, black pepper and chilli flakes and add salt to taste. You might prefer more of the numbing heat of the Sichuan pepper or more heat from the chilli. Keep to one side.

Mix 1 tsp of the spice mix into the cornflour.

Clean the prawns to your preference. They can be peeled and deveined, or cut through the shell with scissors and devein leaving the shell on.

Toss the prawns, the spring onions and garlic through the cornflour mix. Shake off any excess and lay out – not touching – on a tray (this can be done ahead).

When ready to cook, pour about 5cm of oil into a large, deep saucepan and heat to 180°C. You can test the temperature by frying a small piece of garlic: it should sizzle instantly and take about 20 seconds to turn golden.

Fry the prawns, in batches, for 1–2 minutes or until golden and crisp. Remove with a slotted spoon, to drain on a baking tray lined with kitchen paper. Sprinkle with more of the spice mix and keep warm while you cook the remaining prawns. Serve immediately.

Peach, Basil, Mozzarella and Rocket Salad

....

This is the perfect summer starter, a classic Italian combination. It is important to use ripe peaches to get the maximum flavour, although as a last resort you can roast any not-quite-ripe-enough peaches with a sprinkle of sugar in a hot oven, until juicy and fragrant. Use melon, cherries or fresh figs in place of peaches – or in winter use thin slices of raw pink rhubarb and peeled slices of orange. Any edible flowers – borage, nasturtiums or sweet violets – are a pretty addition too. The secret of this salad is in the simplicity of its ingredients, all tip top and at their seasonal best.

SERVES 6

Extra virgin olive oil,
   to drizzle
3 ripe peaches, quartered
4 x 125g buffalo mozzarella
   balls, torn into bite-sized
   pieces
3 big handfuls of rocket
Small bunch of basil or mint,
   leaves picked off
100g sliced prosciutto
   (optional), torn into strips
6 slices of sourdough bread,
   to serve (optional)

Dressing
1 small shallot or ½ small red
   onion, very thinly sliced
2 tbsp red wine vinegar
6 tbsp extra virgin olive oil
Salt and freshly ground
   black pepper

Mix all the dressing ingredients together, season to taste and put to one side.

Toast the bread (if using) just before you make the salad, and drizzle with olive oil.

Arrange the peaches and mozzarella on plates or a big platter and drizzle with half the dressing. Scatter the rocket and herbs over the top and season with a little salt and pepper. If using prosciutto, arrange it over the top and drizzle over the rest of the dressing.

Serve with the toasted sourdough on the side.

Scallops with Jerusalem Artichoke and Hazelnut Butter

This has the look of a well-made restaurant dish, with multiple components, flavours and textures. Here's the trick: with the artichoke purée and the toasted hazelnuts prepared in advance, this dish is simply a matter of searing the scallops, reheating the purée and assembling everything on the plate.

SERVES 6

250g Jerusalem artichokes, peeled and cut into 2cm pieces
50ml milk
100ml double cream
2 tsp chopped fresh thyme
Salt and freshly ground black pepper
30g skinned hazelnuts, roughly chopped or crushed
40g butter
Finely grated zest and juice of 1 lemon
6 very thin slices of pancetta or streaky bacon (optional), roughly chopped
1 tbsp vegetable oil
18 large scallops
Small handful of flat-leaf parsley, radicchio or rocket, roughly chopped

Put the artichokes in a saucepan with the milk, cream, a pinch of the thyme and a pinch of salt. Simmer for 15–20 minutes, stirring occasionally, until the artichokes are tender.

Transfer the contents of the pan to a food processor or blender and blend until smooth, adding salt and pepper to taste. Keep warm, or keep to one side to reheat.

Fry the hazelnuts with three-quarters of the butter until the butter foams and starts to turn golden brown. Remove from the heat and add a good squeeze of lemon juice, some lemon zest and the rest of the thyme. Keep warm, or keep to one side to reheat.

If using pancetta or bacon, fry until really crisp and browned, then put to one side on kitchen paper.

When ready to serve, make sure the artichoke purée and hazelnuts are warm; heat a large frying pan over medium heat and add about 1 tablespoon of oil. Season the scallops with salt, then carefully place in the pan, without overcrowding them.

Cook for 1–2 minutes until nicely seared, then flip them over in the order in which you put them in the pan. Add the rest of the butter and cook for another 1–2 minutes, carefully spooning the foaming butter over the scallops. Add a squeeze of lemon juice, then transfer to a plate to rest for a minute.

Spoon the Jerusalem artichoke purée on to warmed plates. Put the scallops on top. Spoon the hazelnut butter over, then scatter over the chopped leaves and bacon (if using). Serve immediately.

Lamb, Radicchio, Fig and Hazelnut Salad

....

Lamb shoulder is a forgiving cut to roast – long and slow, it is almost impossible to go wrong. For this dish, the meat is best served just warm – too cold and the fat will set, too hot and the rocket will wilt. Cook the lamb late in the afternoon and have the joint covered and resting in the hour or two before supper is served. Kick back and think about knocking out some cocktails. If fresh figs are unavailable, use roughly chopped medjool dates or plump dried figs (a little extra lemon juice in the dressing might be needed to balance out the sweetness).

SERVES 6

(add about 150g lamb, some chicory and/or radicchio and a few figs for each extra person)

1.5kg bone-in lamb shoulder
  or lamb shanks
4 tbsp olive oil
2 tsp chopped fresh thyme
  or rosemary
Salt and freshly ground
  black pepper
2 small radicchio, thickly
  sliced
3 chicory, thickly sliced
15 fresh ripe figs, halved
Big handful of rocket
Big handful of roasted
  hazelnuts, walnuts or
  almonds

Dressing
80ml olive oil
4 tbsp red wine vinegar or
  lemon juice
1 tbsp honey
1 tsp chopped fresh thyme
  or rosemary

Preheat the oven to 150°C (140°C fan).

Rub the lamb with 1 tablespoon of the olive oil and the thyme and season with salt and pepper. Put the lamb in a roasting tin, skin-side up, and cover the tin with foil. Roast for 4–5 hours, regularly basting the meat with the cooking juices.

When the lamb is completely tender, remove from the oven and leave to rest for 15 minutes, or until ready to serve. Strain the cooking juices and reserve.

Cut or pull the lamb into bite-sized pieces, discarding any fatty pieces, and set aside in a warm place. You can also keep the lamb in the fridge for a day or so, frying in pieces to warm through.

Turn the oven up to 200°C (190°C fan).

Put the radicchio and chicory on a baking tray, add 2 tablespoons of olive oil and season with salt and pepper; bake in the oven for about 15 minutes, until just tender and beginning to caramelise.

Put the figs in a bowl, add a pinch of salt and 1 tablespoon of olive oil and mix gently. Place on a baking tray and cook in the oven for 5 minutes, or until they start to soften. Remove.

For the dressing, whisk all the ingredients together with salt and pepper to taste and set aside.

To serve, lay half the figs, the chicory and radicchio on a large platter and top with the warm lamb, a few tablespoons of the cooking juices and the dressing. Top with the remaining figs and scatter with the rocket and nuts and serve at once.

Slow-Baked Salmon with Spring Vegetables and Lemon Butter

This method of cooking salmon, or large trout, is perfect for a dinner party, as you can cook the fish and vegetables before people arrive and hurl everything together later on. The vegetables can be adjusted according to what is in season. Any leftover fish can be mixed with a little mayonnaise for a great sandwich filling or served with a salad.

SERVES 6
(add about 150g fish and some vegetables for each extra person)

1 centre cut (the thickest section) of salmon or large trout fillet (about 1kg)
Extra virgin olive oil
Salt and freshly ground black pepper
1 shallot, finely chopped
Finely grated zest and juice of 1 lemon
Big bunch of fresh herbs (tarragon, chervil or parsley), leaves and stalks separated and roughly chopped

Vegetables
375g green beans
150g asparagus tips
225g sugar snap peas, trimmed (or peas)
40g butter

Preheat the oven to 90°C (or as low as it will go) and place a baking dish half filled with boiling water in the bottom of the oven.

Brush the fish all over with a little olive oil and place on a baking tray. Season generously with salt and pepper, then top with the shallot, lemon zest and the chopped herb stalks.

Bake the fish in the low oven for about 30–40 minutes. You can tell the salmon is done when it feels just firm to the touch and white juices are just starting to break through the surface. You can either leave the salmon to rest for 10 minutes, then serve, or cover it with foil and leave to rest for up to 2 hours before serving.

For the vegetables, bring a large pan of salted water to the boil, add the green beans and cook for 3 minutes, then add the asparagus tips and cook for 3 minutes more. Add the sugar snap peas and cook for 1 minute, then thoroughly drain the vegetables and either return to the pan or rinse under cold water and put aside to reheat later.

When ready to serve, warm the vegetables in the butter, add lemon juice and salt and pepper to taste and stir through the herbs until all the vegetables are evenly coated.

Gently brush the herbs and shallots off the salmon and add a squeeze of lemon juice. Pull into large flakes and put on to a big platter or plates.

Spoon over the vegetables and buttery juices from the pan and serve.

Saltimbocca

Saltimbocca is an Italian dish: the name loosely translates rather charmingly as 'jump in the mouth'. It's pretty quick to cook if the preparation has all been done beforehand, and the Parma ham and sage flavour the meat as it fries in the pan. Do try to source English rose veal, or ensure that any veal you buy has the highest welfare standard. Serve with sautéed or roasted potatoes and a simple salad or green vegetables.

SERVES 6

(add an escalope, plus
2 sage leaves and 2 slices
of prosciutto, for each
extra person)

6 x 150g veal or pork
   escalopes
12 sage leaves
Salt and freshly ground
   black pepper
12 slices of prosciutto
   (Parma ham is best)
2–3 tbsp plain flour
1 tbsp olive oil
3 tbsp unsalted butter
2 garlic cloves, slightly
   flattened with the side of
   a knife
200ml dry Marsala wine or
   dry white wine (optional)

Place the meat between two pieces of clingfilm or greaseproof paper and flatten to about 5mm, using a meat mallet or a rolling pin. Cut each escalope in half, stick a sage leaf to each piece and give a nice grind of pepper. Wrap each piece of meat in prosciutto and dust lightly in flour.

Heat the oil and butter in a large frying pan over a medium heat. Add the garlic and let it sizzle, then add the meat and cook for 2 minutes on each side, until golden and cooked through. Remove and keep warm on a serving dish.

If you want to make a sauce, add the Marsala to the pan and bubble it over a high heat until thickened and reduced by half. Taste for seasoning, remove the garlic and serve the sauce poured over the meat.

Baked Duck Legs with Spiced Plums

This Chinese-inspired duck dish should go down a storm with its bold flavours and rich colours. Duck legs are a great option for dinner parties: impressively different, they are surprisingly economical to buy and (here's the best bit) are quite happy being cooked an hour or so in advance, then reheated. By all means use the same flavourings to marinate and cook firm tofu if you have any vegetarian guests; just reduce the cooking time to about 20 minutes in total and cook uncovered from the start, until the sauce is rich and thick.

SERVES 6
(add 1 duck leg
and a few plums for
each extra person)

2 tsp five spice
3 star anise
3 tbsp soy sauce
½ cinnamon stick
1 bay leaf
1 red chilli, deseeded and
	chopped
1 tbsp honey
6 large duck legs
1 mandarin or small orange,
	peel (no white pith)
	removed in long strips
1 tbsp white wine vinegar
4 thin slices of fresh ginger
20–24 plums, halved and
	stoned
Brown or white rice, to serve
Steamed or boiled greens,
	to serve

Mix together the five spice, star anise, soy sauce, cinnamon, bay, chilli and honey. Add the duck legs and rub all over with the marinade, then put in the fridge for at least 2 hours or overnight.

Preheat the oven to 180°C (170°C fan).

Place the duck legs in a roasting tin or large casserole with the juice of the mandarin or orange, tightly cover with foil or a lid, and cook for 1 hour.

Remove from the oven and stir through the vinegar, ginger, mandarin or orange peel and the plums. Return to the oven uncovered, turn the oven down to 160°C (150°C fan) and cook for 1–1½ hours, until the duck is tender and falling off the bone and you have a rich and sticky sauce. Add a tiny splash of water during cooking if the sauce is drying out too much.

Keep covered until ready to serve; if necessary, reheat in a low oven while you cook the rice and greens.

BAKES

The weekend isn't complete without at least one cake, biscuit or bake emerging from the oven, filling the house with a glorious, sweet smell. Baking is hands-down one of the most relaxing ways to spend time in the kitchen; an activity that cannot be rushed. Whether you are baking for a teatime spread complete with great big pot of tea, or for a pudding to serve with a dollop of cream, these recipes will remind you why baking is such a special treat. Apron at the ready!

Ham, Cheese and Olive Loaf

A good savoury cake or loaf is a fine thing. This one eats terrifically when freshly cooked and straight from the tin; toasted, it will make a wonderful snack. Omit the ham if you'd like a vegetarian version; the olives give memorable salty bursts but aren't essential if you'd rather leave them out. Switch herbs around too, if you like. This is more of a method for savoury bread than a finite recipe.

MAKES 8 SLICES

250g plain flour
2 tsp baking powder
Salt and freshly ground
    black pepper
2 tsp finely chopped
    rosemary or thyme leaves
4 eggs, beaten
150ml milk
100ml dry white wine or
    water
100ml olive oil, plus extra
    for greasing
200g cooked ham, finely
    chopped
200g cheese, grated
150g green olives, pitted and
    roughly chopped
3 spring onions, finely
    chopped

Preheat the oven to 200°C (190°C fan). Line a 1.5-litre loaf tin with baking parchment and brush with olive oil.

Sift the flour with the baking powder into a large mixing bowl. Add ½ teaspoon each of salt and pepper and add the herbs.

Beat together the eggs, milk and wine. Make a well in the centre of the flour mix and gently stir in the egg mixture, just until combined.

Add the olive oil a little at a time, mixing until the batter is smooth, then add the ham, cheese, olives and spring onions and gently mix, just until incorporated.

Pour the batter into the prepared tin and bake for about 1 hour, until golden brown and a skewer inserted deep into the centre of the cake comes out clean. If it is browning too much towards the end of baking time, cover with foil.

Leave to cool in the tin for 10 minutes, then turn out on to a wire rack and cool for another 10–15 minutes before slicing.

Filled Thumbprint Biscuits

Making your own biscuits really cements what is special about that age-old union of a cup of tea and a biscuit. Invite someone round, stick the kettle on and whip out a plate of freshly made biscuits. Friends for life, no doubt! These thumbprint biscuits will show off any jams you might have to hand.

MAKES ABOUT 18 BISCUITS

120g butter, at room temperature
70g light muscovado or soft brown sugar
120g plain or wholemeal flour
60g ground almonds
Raspberry or cherry jam (or whatever flavour you prefer)

Using a mixer, cream together the butter and sugar until light and fluffy.

Stir the flour and almonds together, then mix into the butter mixture to form a dough. Wrap and put in the fridge for 30 minutes.

Preheat the oven to 180°C (170°C fan) and line a baking sheet with baking parchment.

Roll heaped tablespoons of the dough into balls and place on the baking sheet; using a wet thumb, make a deep indentation in the centre of each ball. Place in the oven for 5 minutes, then carefully remove from the oven and press again if any of the thumbprints have disappeared. Fill each biscuit with a scant teaspoon of jam.

Bake for a further 5 minutes, or until the edges are just golden brown, then place on a wire rack to cool.

Magic Cake

Magic cakes are made from a simple batter, cooked at a low temperature. Here's the magic – the cake divides into three layers as it cooks: layer one is a dense, moist base; layer two is a delicate creamy middle; and layer three is a light sponge top. More than other cake recipes, it is important to use the right-sized tin; using the wrong-sized tin will mean the layers won't work properly, losing their magic. Once you've mastered the method, this is a good recipe to experiment with flavouring: using different fruits and cordials, adding cocoa powder with the flour, replacing the lemon juice with a little extra milk, or using rum instead of the cordial.

MAKES ABOUT 10 SLICES

350ml milk
Finely grated zest and juice
  of 1 large lemon (around
  50ml juice)
4 eggs, separated
160g caster sugar, plus extra
  to sprinkle
125g butter, melted
115g self-raising flour
50ml elderflower cordial

Preheat the oven to 150°C (140°C fan). Line a 24-cm round springclip tin with baking parchment.

Warm the milk with the lemon zest and put to one side to infuse.

Using an electric whisk or mixer, whisk the egg yolks with the sugar until pale. Add the butter and lemon juice and whisk for a minute or two, until combined.

Sift in the flour and gently fold it in.

Slowly start whisking the milk into the batter, followed by the elderflower cordial.

In a very clean bowl, whisk the egg whites until stiff. Add a big spoonful of the whisked whites to the cake batter to loosen it, then gently stir in the remainder a little at a time. Don't overmix; you will still see bits of egg whites in the batter, but this is fine.

Pour the batter into the cake tin and bake for 40 minutes or until the top is lightly browned, although it will be slightly wobbly. Sprinkle with a little more sugar and leave to cool in the tin.

Place the tin in the fridge to set for at least 2 hours before removing the cake from the tin.

Brioche Ice Cream Sandwiches

Totally indulgent, brioche is bread made milky, buttery heaven. Not only does this recipe have you baking your own brioche (take a quick bow), it then has you stuffing it with ice cream coated with raspberries and chopped nuts. The stuff of desert island dreams, surely?

MAKES 8
(you can freeze excess buns)

125ml warm water
1 tsp dried yeast (not fast-
    action)
1 tbsp whole milk
1 tbsp soft light brown sugar
30g cold butter, diced
Pinch of salt
225g strong white flour,
    plus extra for dusting
1 large egg, beaten, plus 1 egg
    yolk, for glazing

Filling
125g frozen (or freeze-dried)
    raspberries
800ml vanilla ice cream
    (or your favourite flavour,
    or use sorbet)
4 tbsp chopped almonds,
    pistachios or hazelnuts

Mix the water, yeast, milk and sugar in a jug and leave to stand for 5 minutes until it froths.

Rub the butter and salt into the flour, using your fingertips or in a food processor, until the mixture resembles fine breadcrumbs.

Make a well in the centre of the flour and add the yeast mixture and the beaten egg. Use your hands to mix it into a sticky and wet dough, then scrape out on to a floured work surface.

Stretch and fold the dough for 5 minutes, adding as little flour as possible, until it feels soft and bouncy. Place in an oiled bowl, cover with clingfilm and set aside to rise for about 1 hour, or until doubled in size.

Line a large baking sheet with baking parchment.

Once the dough has doubled in size, knock the air out and knead again for 2 minutes. Divide the dough into eight equal pieces. Roll into balls and arrange on the lined baking sheet. Loosely cover with oiled clingfilm and leave for about 1 hour, or until doubled in size again.

Preheat the oven to 200°C (190°C fan) and place a small baking tray in the bottom of the oven.

Brush the buns with egg yolk and pour a cup of water into the baking tray in the bottom of the oven to create steam. Bake the buns for 20 minutes, or until golden, then leave to cool on a wire rack.

While the brioche is cooking, chop the raspberries while still frozen (defrost a tiny bit if needed), then return to the freezer.

Soften the ice cream enough to shape into eight balls, then coat in the raspberries, flattening slightly to a burger shape, and return to the freezer.

When the brioche buns are cold, split them, insert the flattened ice cream ball, sprinkle with the nuts and eat.

Apple and Oat Cake

Hot from the oven, apple cakes represent a time when the apple trees hang heavy and autumn is well and truly under way. Many's the time I've had a bag of apples given to me by a friend lucky enough to have their own tree. This apple cake keeps exceptionally well and uses oats in place of some of the flour. Serve on the day it is baked, still warm, as the perfect autumnal pudding alongside some vanilla ice cream, crème fraîche or whipped cream. Cold, it makes a great lunch box addition.

MAKES ABOUT 8 SLICES

100g rolled oats, plus extra
    to sprinkle
85g plain flour
1½ tsp baking powder
1 vanilla pod, seeds scraped
    out (or use 1 tsp ground
    cinnamon)
250g caster sugar, plus extra
    to sprinkle
2 eggs
110g melted butter, plus
    extra for greasing
150ml milk
Finely grated zest of 1 lemon
2 dessert apples, peeled,
    cored and thinly sliced

Preheat the oven to 180°C (170°C fan). Line an approximately 24-cm round cake tin with baking parchment and grease with butter.

Whizz the oats in a blender or food processor for a few seconds, to create a coarse flour, then mix with the plain flour and baking powder.

Mix the vanilla seeds or cinnamon with the sugar. Beat the eggs in a bowl, add the flavoured sugar and beat until thick and light.

Slowly add the melted butter and milk to the egg mixture, and then fold in the flour mix to make a batter. Add the lemon zest and half the apples to the batter.

Pour into the prepared tin, put the remaining apples on the top, and sprinkle with 1 tablespoon of sugar and a few oats.

Bake for 1 hour, or until a skewer inserted into the centre of the cake comes out clean. Leave to cool in the tin for about 20 minutes before serving, or turning out on to a wire rack to cool.

Peanut and Chocolate Fudge

Fudge is the guilty pleasure many of us find hard to ignore. This recipe is turbocharged fudge, with dark chunks of chocolate and peanuts in the mix. Add a pinch of flaky sea salt and you're on track for a grown-up and contemporary sweet treat.

MAKES 30 SMALL SQUARES

120g unsalted butter
Pinch of ground cinnamon, nutmeg or mixed spice
450g light muscovado or soft dark brown sugar
120ml milk
220g crunchy peanut butter
300g icing sugar, sifted
80g dark chocolate, broken into small pieces
Flaky or coarse sea salt (optional)

Line a 20cm square cake tin with clingfilm or baking parchment.

Melt the butter with the spices in a large saucepan. Stir in the brown sugar and milk and bring to the boil; boil for 2 minutes without stirring. Remove from the heat and stir in the peanut butter.

Put the icing sugar in a large mixing bowl. Pour in the hot peanut butter mixture and beat until smooth.

Pour the fudge into the lined tin, cover the top with clingfilm or baking parchment, and smooth the top. Leave to cool slightly for 10 minutes, then place in the fridge to cool completely.

Remove the top layer of clingfilm or parchment.

Put a heatproof bowl over a small pan of water over a medium heat (do not let the bottom of the bowl touch the water). Add the chocolate and stir until smooth and melted. Spread a thin layer of chocolate over the fudge. Leave the chocolate to cool slightly. Sprinkle the top with a few flakes of sea salt (if using), then leave to cool completely.

Carefully lift the fudge out of the tin on to a board and cut into about 30 squares.

Store in an airtight container.

Florentines

Despite their name, florentines are actually a French rather than Italian biscuit. Crisp and rich, I would urge you to make your own. I cook these in a slab, then drizzle with melted chocolate before cutting into individual squares. Best eaten on the day they are made for a superior texture, florentines will keep well enough in an airtight tin for a good few days – though I can't imagine a scenario where florentines didn't get gobbled immediately.

**MAKES ABOUT
20–24 SQUARES**

50g butter
50 light muscovado sugar
50g honey
2 tbsp plain flour
75ml crème fraîche or
    sour cream
50g flaked almonds
20g desiccated coconut
30g candied peel
60g dried sour cherries or
    cranberries
150g good-quality dark
    chocolate, broken into
    pieces

Preheat the oven to 180°C (170°C fan) and line a 30 x 20cm baking tray with baking parchment.

Heat the butter, sugar and honey in a saucepan over a medium heat, stirring continuously until the sugar has dissolved.

In a small bowl, beat the flour and crème fraîche together, then beat into the butter mix. Add the almonds, coconut, candied peel and dried cherries and mix well until combined.

Spread the florentine mixture in a very thin layer in the lined tray and bake for about 10–12 minutes, until a rich golden colour.

Leave in the tin to cool and firm up for about 10 minutes. Then turn out on to a wire rack so the flat side is uppermost.

Put a heatproof bowl over a small pan of water over a medium heat (do not let the bottom of the bowl touch the water). Add the chocolate and stir until smooth and melted. Drizzle the chocolate over the florentine and leave until just set. Cut into squares and leave to cool completely. Store in an airtight container.

Stout, Oat and Chocolate Cake

This deeply flavoured, dense and chocolatey cake is very satisfying to make and, of course, to eat. Each ingredient flatters the other and this cake eats better after a day or so. It's the sort of cake you take away for a long weekend with friends; it's the sort of cake that will make you friends. Serve with a thick slick of cream or a tart blob of crème fraîche or sour cream.

MAKES 12 SLICES

250ml stout
230g unsalted butter
70g unsweetened cocoa
    powder
50g rolled oats
200g plain flour
250g light brown or golden
    caster sugar
1½ tsp bicarbonate of soda
Big pinch of salt
2 eggs, beaten
150g sour cream or crème
    fraîche, plus extra to serve

Caramelised oats

2 tbsp rolled oats
1 tbsp light brown or golden
    caster sugar

Preheat the oven to 180°C (170°C fan) and line a 24-cm round cake tin with baking parchment.

Bring the stout and butter to the boil in a large saucepan over a medium heat. Add the cocoa powder and oats and whisk until smooth. Remove from the heat.

Whisk together the flour, sugar, bicarbonate of soda and salt in a large bowl.

Whisk the eggs and sour cream into the stout and cocoa mixture until completely combined. Add the flour mixture and fold together until the batter is completely combined. Pour the batter into the prepared tin and bake for about 45 minutes, or until a skewer inserted into the centre of the cake comes out clean.

While the cake is baking, prepare the caramelised oats: toast the oats and sugar together in a dry pan until golden brown and the sugar is starting to caramelise. Scrape on to a plate to cool. Put to one side or store in a small airtight container.

When the cake is cooked, transfer the tin to a wire rack and leave to cool completely, then turn the cake out on to the rack. Store in an airtight container.

To serve, partially crush the caramelised oats with a mortar and pestle or a rolling pin. Slice the cake and serve with sour cream, sprinkling the caramelised oats over the top.

Walnut Cake

If you have a food processor, then this cake can be thrown together in no time at all. Even if you don't have one, it's still worth the effort because the recipe is super easy to assemble. The cake has two layers: a crisp sandy base and a spongy top, dense and laden with toasted walnuts. Use almonds or hazelnuts if you prefer. This cake is best eaten on the day it is made, or even still slightly warm.

MAKES 8–10 SLICES

100g walnuts, roughly
  chopped
130g light brown sugar, plus
  2 tbsp to sprinkle
100g plain flour
1 tsp ground cinnamon
Pinch of salt
50g cold butter, diced
120ml sour cream, plus extra
  to serve
½ tsp baking powder
1 egg

Preheat the oven to 180°C (170°C fan) and line a 24-cm round springclip tin with greaseproof paper.

Use a food processor or rolling pin to crush half the walnuts to a coarse powder. Mix the sugar, flour, cinnamon and salt into the walnut powder.

Rub the butter into the flour mix by pulsing in a food processor or using your fingertips, until you have a sandy texture. Spread half this mix into the cake tin and press down slightly to form an even base.

Whisk together the sour cream, baking powder and egg. Add this to the remaining flour mix, then pour over the base. Sprinkle the mix with the rest of the chopped walnuts and 2 tablespoons of sugar.

Bake for 40 minutes, until golden on top and a skewer inserted into the centre of the cake comes out clean. Leave to cool in the tin for 15–20 minutes, then remove and leave on a wire rack to cool. Slice and serve with sour cream.

Spiced-Coffee Meringue

Coffee works wonderfully with meringue, with the coffee all bitter and rich, complementing the clean sweetness of the meringue. Do not overcook the meringue so that it is crisp, or it will fall apart as you roll it, making the cake tricky to assemble. Don't be too anxious, though: this type of cake should have a charmingly unorderly finished look! As with all meringues, make sure the bowl and whisk are both completely clean before you begin whisking the egg whites.

SERVES 8

Sunflower oil, for greasing
350g golden or white caster
  sugar
6 egg whites
½ tsp ground cinnamon
½ tsp ground cardamom
2 tbsp strong espresso or
  1 tbsp coffee powder
  dissolved in 1 tbsp boiling
  water
60g flaked almonds, plus a
  handful to sprinkle
150g good-quality dark
  chocolate (70% cocoa),
  chopped into small pieces,
  plus 50g to drizzle
40g unsalted butter
300ml double cream

Preheat the oven to 200°C (190°C fan). Line a 20 x 30cm Swiss roll tin or baking tray with baking parchment, then lightly oil the paper. Put 300g of the sugar on the lined tray and put in the oven for 5 minutes.

In a large clean bowl, using an electric mixer, whisk the egg whites until thick, glossy and holding firm, but not stiff, peaks. On a low speed, whisk in the hot sugar, a little at a time, and continue to whisk until stiff and glossy, then fold in the spices and three-quarters of the coffee, until just combined.

Spread the meringue evenly into the lined tin, scatter over the flaked almonds, then bake for 8 minutes.

Turn the oven down to 160°C (150°C fan) and cook for a further 10–15 minutes, until the centre is cooked but still soft. Using the paper, lift the meringue from the tin on to a wire rack and cool for 10 minutes, then invert on to a big chopping board.

Put a heatproof bowl over a small pan of water over a medium heat (do not let the bottom of the bowl touch the water). Add 150g of the chocolate and stir until smooth and melted. Gently stir in the butter, followed by 100ml of the cream, then leave to cool for 5 minutes.

Spread the chocolate mix evenly over the cooled meringue, then chill the dessert for 15 minutes.

Put the remaining 200ml of cream, the remaining 50g of sugar and the remaining coffee in a clean mixing bowl and whisk to soft peaks. Spread the cream on top of the chocolate spread.

Starting with a short edge, carefully roll up the meringue, using the baking paper to help. Wrap the paper tightly around and chill for at least 2 hours.

To serve, put on a plate, melt the remaining 50g chocolate and drizzle over the roll, then sprinkle with flaked almonds.

Whole Lemon Pie

Lemons make for wonderful puddings. A burst of citrus matched with something creamy and sweet is a classic combination. This recipe uses whole lemons to give an extra juicy lemony thwack. Do try to find unwaxed lemons. As a last resort, use waxed lemons: first run them under some warm water and then gently scrub with a wire wool brush to remove any residual wax. This lemon tart is best served at room temperature.

2 unwaxed lemons, cut into very thin slices and any pips removed

300g white sugar, plus 1 tbsp to sprinkle

3 eggs

2 tbsp plain flour

100g butter, melted

Pastry (or use 600g shortcrust pastry)

300g plain flour, plus extra for dusting

2 tsp caster sugar

Salt

150g butter, very cold, cut into 2cm cubes

80ml ice-cold water

1 tbsp milk

Place the lemon slices in a mixing bowl and toss with the sugar. Cover and leave to macerate at room temperature for at least 2 hours, or overnight.

To make the pastry: put the flour, sugar and salt into a mixing bowl or food processor, then rub in the butter until it resembles coarse sand. Drizzle in the water in several additions, pulsing or mixing until the dough starts to come together, trying not to overwork the dough. Gather the dough into two balls, flatten into discs, wrap and put in the fridge for at least 30 minutes.

Preheat the oven to 220°C (200°C fan) and line a 23cm tart tin with greaseproof paper.

Unwrap a disc of dough, place between two sheets of clingfilm and roll out to a 25cm circle. Lay it on a baking sheet, cover and chill in the fridge while you roll the second disc to a 23cm circle. Gently place the larger circle in the tart tin, letting the dough rise up the sides (do not trim). Cover and chill in the fridge.

Vigorously mix the eggs, 2 tablespoons of flour and the melted butter into the lemon and sugar mixture. Pour the mixture into the dough-lined tart tin to just below the tin's rim.

Lay the small dough circle on top of the filling, and cut four small holes. Squeeze together the edges of the top and bottom dough circles. Brush with milk and sprinkle with 1 tablespoon of sugar. Bake for 30 minutes, then reduce the heat to 180°C (170°C fan) and bake for a further 20 minutes.

Leave to completely cool to room temperature before serving.

Salted Caramel Brownies

Salted caramel is omnipresent these days, and for good reason: a bit of salt enhances the flavour of caramel no end. I like to swirl the caramel through the mixture, leaving thick blobs of it remaining in the cooked brownie. Cocoa nibs intensify chocolate flavour and are brilliant for adding texture; they are available in health food shops and some larger supermarkets.

**MAKES 20 SMALL
BUT RICH SQUARES**

Caramel
75g white caster sugar
50ml double cream
10g butter
Pinch of sea salt flakes

Brownies
100g butter
100g caster sugar
150g light brown sugar
75g golden syrup
300g good-quality dark
    chocolate (70% cocoa),
    broken into small pieces
4 eggs, beaten
70g plain flour or rye flour
3 tbsp cocoa nibs or chopped
    nuts (optional)

First, make the caramel. Sprinkle the sugar in an even layer in a heavy-based pan over a medium heat. Do not stir. When the edges start to liquefy, very gently tilt the pan to move the melted sugar around on to the dry spots until all the sugar is liquid.

Turn up the heat a bit and continue cooking until the caramel is deep golden brown. Immediately remove from the heat and gradually whisk in the cream, taking care as it will bubble vigorously. Add the butter and the salt and stir until smooth. Pour into a bowl to cool.

Preheat the oven to 160°C (150°C fan) and line a 23-cm square cake tin with baking parchment.

To make the brownies, melt the butter, sugars and golden syrup in a pan, then beat until smooth. Take off the heat, add the chocolate and stir gently until melted and smooth.

Mix in the eggs, then the flour, and beat until smooth and glossy. Pour into the prepared tin.

Drizzle the cooled caramel over the mix, then use a skewer or knife tip to gently swirl the caramel through the chocolate mix. Sprinkle the cocoa nibs or nuts over the top. Bake for 20 minutes.

Remove from the oven and leave to cool in the tin, then chill in the fridge for at least 1 hour.

Cut into pieces using a sharp knife dipped into hot water and cleaned between each cut. Serve cold or at room temperature.

Conversions

WEIGHTS

7.5g	¼oz
15g	½oz
20g	¾oz
30g	1oz
35g	1¼oz
40g	1½oz
50g	1¾oz
55g	2oz
60g	2¼oz
70g	2½oz
80g	2¾oz
85g	3oz
90g	3¼oz
100g	3½oz
115g	4oz
125g	4½oz
140g	5oz
150g	5½oz
170g	6oz
185g	6½oz
200g	7oz
225g	8oz
250g	9oz
285g	10oz
300g	10½oz
310g	11oz
340g	12oz
370g	13oz
400g	14oz
425g	15oz
450g	1lb
500g	1lb 2oz
565g	1¼ lb
680g	1½ lb
700g	1lb 9oz
750g	1lb 10oz
800g	1¾ lb
900g	2lb
1kg	2lb 3oz
1.1kg	2lb 7oz
1.4kg	3lb
1.5kg	3½lb
1.8kg	4lb
2kg	4½lb
2.3kg	5lb
2.7kg	6lb
3.1kg	7lb
3.6kg	8lb
4.5kg	10lb

VOLUME

5ml	1 teaspoon	
10ml	1 dessertspoon	
15ml	1 tablespoon	
30ml	1fl oz	
40ml	1½fl oz	
55ml	2fl oz	
70ml	2½fl oz	
85ml	3fl oz	
100ml	3½ fl oz	
120ml	4fl oz	
130ml	4½fl oz	
150ml	5fl oz	
170ml	6fl oz	
185ml	6½fl oz	
200ml	7fl oz	
225ml	8fl oz	
250ml	9fl oz	
270ml	9½fl oz	
285ml	10fl oz	½ pint
300ml	10½fl oz	
345ml	12fl oz	
400ml	14fl oz	
425ml	15fl oz	¾ pint
450ml	16fl oz	
465ml	16½fl oz	
500ml	18fl oz	
565ml	20fl oz	1 pint
700ml	25fl oz	1¼ pints
750ml	26fl oz	
850ml	30fl oz	1½ pints
1 litre	35fl oz	1¾ pints
1.2 litres	38½fl oz	2 pints
1.5 litres	53fl oz	2½ pints
2 litres	70fl oz	3½ pints

All eggs are medium unless stated otherwise. Use either metric or imperial measures, not a mixture of the two.

LENGTH

5mm	¼in
1cm	½in
2cm	¾in
2.5cm	1in
6cm	2½in
7cm	2¾in
7.5cm	3in
9cm	3½in
10cm	4in
18cm	7in
20cm	8in
22cm	8½in
23cm	9in
25cm	10in
28cm	11in
30cm	12in
35cm	14in
38cm	15in

Oven Temperatures

DESCRIPTION	FAN	CONVENTIONAL	GAS
Very cool	100°C	110°C/225°F	Gas ¼
Very cool	120°C	130°C/250°F	Gas ½
Cool	130°C	140°C/275°F	Gas 1
Slow	140°C	150°C/300°F	Gas 2
Moderately slow	150°C	160°C/320°F	Gas 3
Moderately slow	160°C	170°C/325°F	Gas 3
Moderate	170°C	180°C/350°F	Gas 4
Moderately hot	180°C	190°C/375°F	Gas 5
Hot	190°C	200°C/400°F	Gas 6
Very hot	200°C	220°C/425°F	Gas 7
Very hot	220°C	230°C/450°F	Gas 8
Hottest	230°C	240°C/475°F	Gas 9

Index

Acknowledgements

With thanks to Claire Thomson for all her help. Thanks to Maggie Ramsay for editing the recipes, Alice Martinelli for recipe testing, and to everyone involved in the photoshoot – Jill Mead, Henrietta Clancy, Linda Berlin, James Parker, Helen Gatherer and Emma Laws.

7/18